P9-CBM-465

KEN REID

ONE
TO
REMEMBER

STORIES FROM
39 MEMBERS
OF THE
NHL'S ONE GOAL CLUB

Copyright © Ken Reid, 2020

Published by ECW Press
665 Gerrard Street East
Toronto, Ontario, Canada M4M 1Y2
416-694-3348 / info@ecwpress.com

All rights reserved. No part of this publication may be
reproduced, stored in a retrieval system, or transmitted
in any form by any process — electronic, mechanical,
photocopying, recording, or otherwise — without the prior
written permission of the copyright owners and ECW Press.
The scanning, uploading, and distribution of this book via the
Internet or via any other means without the permission of
the publisher is illegal and punishable by law. Please purchase
only authorized electronic editions, and do not participate in
or encourage electronic piracy of copyrighted materials. Your
support of the author's rights is appreciated.

Editor for the Press: Michael Holmes
Cover design: Michel Vrana
Cover and interior images: Ice: © istockphoto.com/letty17
Hockey puck: © istockphoto.com/francisblack

LIBRARY AND ARCHIVES CANADA CATALOGUING IN
PUBLICATION

Title: One to remember : stories from 39 members
of the NHL's one goal club / Ken Reid.

Names: Reid, Ken, 1974– author.

Identifiers: Canadiana (print) 20200235001
Canadiana (ebook) 20200235028

ISBN 978-1-77041-514-0 (softcover)
ISBN 978-1-77305-571-8 (PDF)
ISBN 978-1-77305-570-1 (EPUB)

Subjects: LCSH: Hockey players—Biography.
LCSH: National Hockey League—History.

Classification: LCC GV848.5.A1 R46 2020
DDC 796.962092/2—dc23

The publication of *One to Remember* has been funded in part by the Government of Canada. *Ce livre est financé en partie par le gouvernement du Canada.* We acknowledge the contribution of the Government of Ontario through the Ontario Book Publishing Tax Credit, and through Ontario Creates for the marketing of this book.

PRINTED AND BOUND IN CANADA

PRINTING: SOLISCO   5   4   3   2   1

MIX
Paper from
responsible sources

FSC
www.fsc.org   FSC® C103304

In memory of Bob Warner, NHL Goal Scorer,
who passed away shortly before the publication of this book.

CONTENTS

COLBY ARMSTRONG *Foreword*

It happens in an instant. But really, the effort that went into it can take years, sometimes even decades. I scored my first NHL goal when I was 23. I was given the opportunity on our Penguins second power-play unit. We were in Atlanta playing against the Thrashers. I was a net front guy, and I was making my way to the front of the crease. Mark Recchi just kind of threw it to the net. The rebound popped back door and I swooped in. It was like I was kind of lost and the defender couldn't find me coming in behind him. The rebound came right to me in the blue paint. Kari Lehtonen reached out to try and make a desperation save and I jarred it top shelf... I went top shelf for my first NHL goal.

There was a picture taken right after I scored. The photographer captured me in the middle of my celly, and I have a huge smile on my face. Now the cool thing about it is, years later, when my son Crusie scored his first minor hockey goal, the tournament photographer snapped a picture of him scoring his first goal. We are doing the exact same things with our arms. Our facial expressions are exactly the same. It is awesome: both pictures, that one of me in Atlanta, and the one of my son Cruise, take me right back to the memory of the first of the 89 goals I scored in the NHL.

I stuck around for 476 NHL regular season games, and another nine in the playoffs. That's longer than most of the guys in this book, but I sure shared the same fear. Every day I was in the NHL I was scared of being sent down to the minors. I was scared even when I was established in the NHL and I had a one-way contract. I was scared at camp every year that I wasn't going to make the team. I was definitely afraid of it being over or of something happening to me. So I appreciated every goal I scored. It was an amazing feeling to score in the NHL, no matter how many times you got to do it. That's why you see guys go bananas. Look at Ovechkin: he clearly loves it. It is the best feeling ever. Whether you've scored one, like the guys in this book, or 894, we all know that feeling.

But what if that goal in Atlanta was my only one? That's the reality for the guys in this book. Their first NHL goal was their last. When I think about my last NHL goal, I get a little confused, a little sad. You're going to find out how the guys in the following pages deal with that fact.

I can tell you this, the joy of seeing a teammate score his first NHL goal is pretty awesome. The professional hockey world is a pretty small one, and I was on the bench when Alain Nasreddine scored his one and only NHL goal. Alain's story is in this book. Alain scored his only NHL marker in his hometown, Montreal. I'm sure a lot of fans that night thought Alain was just a guy on the roster. But for those of us on the Pens he meant so much more. He was a journeyman battler, and he'd showed a lot of us the ropes when we played in the AHL. I remember playing soccer, getting loose with Alain and the boys before one of our AHL games early in my pro career. Naz was older than the rest of us, and he worked so hard. One of our teammates, Ramzi Abid, would chirp Naz during our little soccer sessions. He'd say, "Naz, he's not a natural, boys. He's not a natural."

But Naz, like a lot of the guys in this book, he got it done. *The hard way.* It was a little bit ugly but he was a gamer. When he scored for us that night in Montreal, the reaction from the guys on our bench was so genuine. Naz was 31 years old! We all knew how much that moment meant to him. And the read Naz made on that play, you're going to love it. I did. And wait until you find out who set up Naz for his only NHL goal. It's a great story about a great guy that I knew and played with. A fan in the stands may not think a guy's lone NHL goal could mean much to the rest of the guys on a team, but trust me, organizational joy was felt from top to bottom. We got such great energy when Naz scored. And that he scored it in is his hometown? It was the perfect setting, like it was supposed to happen — storybook stuff. I'm glad his story ended up in here. I love that guy.

If Naz was not a natural, then a guy like Darren Haydar was. Haydar was a sick player. He was maybe unheard of at the National Hockey League level, but he absolutely crushed it in the American League. It was like it was easy for him. There are so many players in this book who were fantastic players, that for whatever reason just couldn't find their way to the NHL. I played against Darren in a Calder Cup Final. He was unreal. He smoked us--he was so good. And Darren's journey to the NHL was not just about hockey. Ken will take you beyond the "Golly gee, it was nice to get one" clichés and let you know the real stories, and sometimes struggles, of what it takes to score at the NHL level.

And yeah, players hear it from fans all the time: "That guy sucks . . . he's a plug." Really? I was on the ice helping instruct some college-aged kids the other day. I was thinking about one of my old teammates. He was a tough guy, but he could play. And I realized, if you were to put him out here . . . he thinks the game 100 miles per hour faster than these kids. He thinks the game so much better than these 17- and 18-year-olds. That tough guy would dominate. He'd be the best player out here. But meanwhile you get a fan out there on social media or in the peanut gallery as you're walking through a parking lot that tells you, "You suck. You don't barely play. You're brutal." No. This book is a testament to just how hard it is to make the NHL.

You're going to read about players you have heard of, and you're going to learn about players whose names you don't recognize. It's an easy, cool read. And once you're done, you'll realize that the way you think about all of these players has changed. You're going to realize that the guy some fans may dismiss because he's someone who "only scored one goal" was much more — an unbelievable teammate or an unbelievable player who turned on the red light just a single time.

— COLBY ARMSTRONG, 2020

Introduction

I'm sure you have a memory of it. It may have been in a city final, it may have been in a house-league game, it may have even been in a game of road hockey. I'm sure you have a memory of that goal you scored.

Now, what if you scored that goal at the game's highest level. What if you scored a goal in the National Hockey League? And what if your goal count ended right there? Would you cherish that moment, or would you want more? That's what I wanted to know when I set out to write this book.

One to Remember is a pretty logical follow up to *One Night Only*. That was a book about men who suited up for a single National Hockey League game. So, here we are a few years later with a book about men who scored a single National Hockey League goal.

Like *One Night Only*, everything behind this book comes from respect. Scoring even a single goal in the greatest hockey league in the world is an incredible feat. Think about the odds you have to defy just to make it onto the ice for an NHL game. In the history of the NHL over sixty-five hundred men have played in at least one shift. And here's the thing: over fifteen hundred men who skated in an NHL game (not counting goalies) never scored. So, it is a grand accomplishment, in my eyes, to light the lamp, even just once.

As I'm sure you will see, just like the men and women in your office, the men in this book all took different paths to reach the pinnacle of their careers. Some of the men in this book were notorious tough guys. Others were highly touted snipers in junior. Some played in the wrong era. For some, their timing was off. For others, their timing was just right. For some, it was a dream.

But was it a dream that didn't last long enough, or a dream that worked out just right?

CHAPTER ONE
THE UNBELIEVABLE

JOHN ENGLISH

Courtesy of the Sault Ste. Marie Greyhounds

There is no magic answer to describe what it is like to score a single goal in the NHL. There are some common themes, but each story has its own individual twist. "It is a little bit wild," John English says.

Consider this twist. John English's tale is a little bit wild. Just over a week after scoring the only goal of his NHL career in a March 30, 1988, 9–7 win for his LA Kings over the Calgary Flames, English was fighting for his life. His hockey stats show that he was out of the game just a year after he scored that goal. Those stats do not say why. "You probably don't know this — so, if you ask why I didn't get a chance to stay, well . . . I broke curfew in the playoffs and ended up getting stabbed and almost dying."

During the Kings' 1988 first-round series against the Flames, English was a healthy scratch for four of the five games. He sat out game one, played in game two and then he and some of the other Black Aces on the team decided to head out for a few pops the night before one of the games English knew he wasn't going to play in. They went to a bar in Marina del Rey, California. They ended up getting into a scrap with another group of guys. The fists flew. "We ended up getting in a fight with some gang guys. We knocked a few of them out, and they came back and stabbed me in the leg when I wasn't looking and hit my femoral artery."

That does not sound good. It was not good. The femoral artery is not a good place to get stabbed. It is loaded with blood. Its primary function is to supply blood to the lower part of your body. Getting stabbed in the femoral artery is a great way to bleed to death.

English was rushed to hospital. He was out of it, but thankfully, he survived. He basically has no memory of what happened after he was stabbed that night. "The nurses told me that Rogie Vachon and Robbie Ftorek came in and talked to me for an hour. I have no recollection of that. I assume it didn't go well because I was traded the next year."

While his Kings teammates went about their playoff series with the Flames, English stayed in the hospital. Calgary eliminated the Kings in five games. English's teammates knew he was in the hospital. They just didn't know which one. The Kings kept things top secret. "It was a pretty good cover-up. They kind of hid me in the hospital for a few weeks. The players didn't really know where I was or anything."

It's amazing how casual John English is when he talks about this incident. I cannot imagine what he went through. He doesn't seem to let it bother him now, and shockingly enough, from the sound of it, it didn't seem to really bother him three decades ago either. "It was very painful. You know what it's like being a 20-year-old guy. It's like, whatever. I didn't really think of it as life and death, even though it was."

Just over a week before his stabbing, English had a meeting with Ftorek that he does remember. It was right after that 9–7 Kings win over the Flames. Aside from scoring his first NHL goal, English also added two assists. The 21-year-old defenceman had three points and was a plus-1 in his NHL debut. But believe it or not, his head coach did not seek him out to heap some praise on the kid. "Ftorek came into the dressing room and kind of tore a strip off of me. Not in front of everybody. He told me he wanted me to play tougher."

Robbie Ftorek wanted the AHL version of English. The six-foot-two 190-pounder had 236 PIMs for New Haven that year. He wanted the tough guy. He did not want the goal scorer. English, despite his three points, was being pigeonholed by the Kings as a tough guy. "I really don't know if that's fair. It's not that I didn't like to fight, but I liked to fight if there was a reason and for my teammates. I wasn't that big of a guy. It wasn't something that I looked forward to."

A little over a week after that night English was stabbed. A year after that he was finished with pro hockey. Why? The answer isn't easy to come by. First, the obvious: "I don't know [if the stabbing had long-lasting effects]. The following year I ended up getting arthritis and getting knocked out [in a fight]. There was some speculation that because I didn't get a blood transfusion [while in hospital] and that when you go through trauma like that, that it can set off the arthritis. At that point, I was just kind of done with hockey, to tell you the truth."

Believe it or not, before the arthritis set in in his leg and shortly after the stabbing, English used the stabbing as a motivator. "It actually motivated me to come back stronger and better the next year because I knew I had screwed up big time."

That motivation did not last. And English says once the arthritis set in, he was pretty much done with the game anyway. He had walked away before, temporarily at least; now he was ready to walk away for good. "I quit when I was 20 and then I came back because I ran out of money. I had spent my signing bonus, so I had to make some money."

Combine the arthritis with perhaps that expectation or that need from his bosses for English to drop the gloves, and you have an early retirement. "I don't want to use that as an excuse, but yes, I would say that at some level . . . I was done with pro hockey." Whatever the reason, John English was finished with pro hockey when he was just 23 years old. He was a kid with a grade 10 education who needed to find out what to do with his life: "I went and worked at a ski resort for a couple of months to pay my mortgage." Then English went into business. He figured that with his lack of education, being an entrepreneur was his only option. "I took my drive as an athlete and turned it around. I was trying to get ahead in life. I've been in the coffee business since I was 24. I own a company now called Oliver's Coffee. It's our own independent chain."

If there is one thing you get from John English when you speak to him it is this: he does not live in the past. He does not have the puck from his single NHL goal. He does not even know where it is. He does not play anymore either. He went for a little skate on a pond a couple of years ago. It was the first time he was on the ice in almost a decade. "That was kind of fun. That's probably not what hockey fans want to hear, but in my case, it's the truth."

"I see some guys that really want to hold on to hockey as their identity, and fair enough. But you can only tell the same stories and live in the past so much. My friends and family are going to get a little bored with me if I keep telling them the same stories from 30 years ago."

But like every player you meet, he does have stories. "I was starting the [his first NHL] game and the national anthem was playing. Ken Baumgartner and Shane Churla were chirping each other and shaking their gloves during the national anthem. They went as soon as the puck was dropped. They dropped their gloves and went at it. That was a little wild. That's one of my bigger memories, actually."

As for his goal, it was on the power play just 94 seconds into the third period. Chris Kontos and Luc Robitaille got the assists. Strangely, the memory of Baumgartner getting ready to fight is a lot clearer in English's mind than what he remembers about his goal: "To be honest I don't have a lot of memories about that goal. The puck got away on me and I shot high. Normally as a defenceman I was always shooting low for tip-ins. I believe I beat the goalie over the glove."

English is not the kind of player you normally read about. That fire within, the "game means everything to me" mentality . . . he didn't have it. But the fact that he played in the NHL, albeit for just a few games, is proof he could play with the best in the world. "I don't diminish having the chance to play a couple of games. That was awesome, especially the culmination. It doesn't start when you're 16. It starts when you're five. I kind of knew, based on my quitting the year before, that my heart wasn't in it that much. I was a high draft pick. I almost felt like I had to play. Getting there and getting my shot and knowing that I could play [in the NHL] makes me feel a little better, I suppose."

John English doesn't often think about scoring in the best hockey league in the world. Could you imagine, just a few days after scoring in the NHL, you get stabbed and you're fighting for your life? He doesn't think much about that either: "I don't even really think about it, to be honest. Just some stories for my friends when we're out for a couple of beers."

CHAPTER TWO

HALL OF FAME HELP

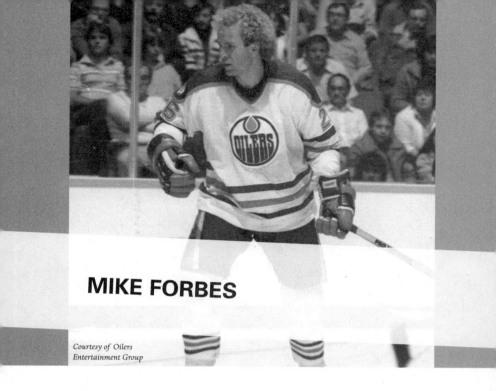

MIKE FORBES

Courtesy of Oilers Entertainment Group

When it comes to the NHL's one goal club, Mike Forbes is as close to royalty as you can get. His lone goal had a couple of notable players pick up the assists: "If I recall correctly, it was Kurri and Gretzky," says Forbes.

You read that correctly: Wayne Gretzky and Jari Kurri assisted on the lone goal of Mike Forbes's NHL career. It came in the 1981–82 season. Wayne Gretzky was on his way to a record 92 goals and a then-record 212 points in a single season. The Oilers were an offensive machine. Forbes, who spent 16 games on the Oilers blue line, found himself on Edmonton's lethal power play on December 5, 1981, in Vancouver. He was locked and loaded and ready to fire: "Gretzky put the puck back to Kurri. Kurri slid it over to me. I one-timed the puck. I got all of it. I rang it off of Glen Hanlon's collarbone. The puck went into the corner."

Now, if we know one thing about the Edmonton Oilers offence in 1981–82, it is this: it was ruthless. The Oilers led the league with 417 goals. A team does not score 417 goals by simply giving up after they rip a shot off of Glen Hanlon's collarbone. Forbes's rebound went right to the one guy you'd want to grab a loose puck. "The puck went into the corner, and who gets it but Gretzky. He sets up the same play again. He tries to come out high and walk the circle. He's denied. He pushes it back to Kurri. Kurri slides it over to me. And this time I don't get all of it. And Hanlon is coming out to cut down the angle. He thinks I'm going to hit him in the collarbone again and he kind of stands up."

A brief interruption here. Somewhere Bobby Hull is smiling. It seems that Forbes wasted the first one: a classic old-school tactic. You shoot high the first time and put a little fear in the goaltender and then slide one along the ice on your next chance. "I got half of it and it slid along ice underneath his stick and between his feet and into the net and I scored my first goal. Yeah, 'wasted the first one and set him up,' I always say."

If you were a member of the Edmonton Oilers in 1981 and you scored your first NHL goal, you didn't think it was going to be your only one. You probably thought you were going to get another one that very night. Those 417 goals the Oilers scored that year were an NHL record for most goals by a team. (In typical Oilers fashion, they broke that record the next year, and then broke that record the following season.) But the one goal that Mike Forbes scored that night was his entire output. "I thought that was going to be the first of many because I was kind of an offensive defencemen. But that wasn't the case."

Forbes struggled to find a permanent spot on the Oilers blue line. He played from time to time with Paul Coffey, but he just couldn't stick. "Garry Lariviere was Paul Coffey's partner. I was supposed to be Paul Coffey's partner when Garry wasn't on or was injured. I was average defensively and I was okay offensively. But if you're going to put somebody with Paul Coffey, you don't need someone who is okay offensively; you need someone who is a defensive, stay-at-home, stalwart defenceman. So, what ended up happening was Garry was injured and I played a couple of games and then I didn't play for a while. It looked like Garry was going to be fine one weekend. They sent me down on a Friday morning."

That was in early January 1982. Forbes boarded a plane and headed for Wichita, Kansas. His orders were to catch up with the Oilers farm team — the CHL's Wichita Wind. While he was in the air, the Oilers were on the phone looking for a replacement for Forbes: "They called up Charlie Huddy, who was my defence partner in Wichita, and Charlie stayed for 20 years. And he deserved it. Charlie was a great player and a great guy. I have nothing but admiration and respect for him, that's just the luck of the draw sometimes. He got a chance to come in and play and kept the job. It is something quite honestly that I never earned. I got a chance to play quite a bit. But there was something about my style of play. Something was missing with that group of people. The management and coaches were looking for something different and they found it in Charlie."

Mike Forbes never played in the NHL again. That goal with the Oilers is not the one that sticks out for Forbes when he thinks of scoring in the NHL, though. Instead, he thinks of a goal he scored a few years earlier when he was playing for Don Cherry's Boston Bruins. It was an exhibition game, so it does not go down in the official record, but for Forbes, it's the goal he thinks of most. "We were playing Philadelphia and George Plimpton played goal for 10 minutes. I'm on the back cover of his book [Open Net]. The game ended up turning into a brawl. I ended up fighting a guy out of the western junior league named Dave Hoyda. Dave had his way with me twice in the same altercation and they broke us up. I went after him a third time and I got a few licks in. I don't know how I didn't get thrown out. At that time, you got three fights and then you got tossed. So, we ended up with a short bench. I think we only had three defencemen and a couple of forwards."

Of course, that meant more ice time for Forbes. And more ice time equals more opportunity. Forbes, just 20 years old, stepped up. "I intercepted a puck at their blue line and I took off down the ice. Bob Dailey was a defenceman for Philly. I was on my right-hand shot on the left wing. I cut across. When I played junior, I always liked to shoot the puck through that defenceman. I ripped a shot through the defenceman's legs over Wayne Stephenson's shoulder. It was a perfect goal, perfect placement. A totally blind shot, so it was all luck."

Forbes and his banged-up body and beat-up face — remember, he had already fought three times that night — headed back to the Bruins bench. "We got the puck and I threw it to Dan Canney, who was the trainer. And Don Cherry came over to me and he said, 'How you feeling, kid?' I said, 'I'm feeling great, Grapes! How do I look?' He said, 'Kid, you look like shit,' because I had been beaten up by Dave Hoyda. That goal is more memorable just because of the interaction at the bench."

Don Cherry was Mike Forbes's kind of guy. Forbes played in the NHL for two legendary coaches: Grapes and Glen Sather. "They're both great hockey guys. Sather was more of a businessman. Always a businessman. Don Cherry was always a player's coach."

Forbes played in 32 games for Cherry's Bruins in 1977–78. He never got an official goal, but he did get four assists. He spent some time in Rochester that year as well, despite Cherry's best efforts. "The Bruins wanted to send me down from Boston to Rochester. Harry [Sinden, Boston's GM] wanted to send me down, and Don called me into the office. He said, 'Mike, Harry wants to send you down to the minors.' I said, 'Okay. When is that going to happen?' He said, 'Maybe tomorrow. You're not supposed to dress tonight, but I'm going to dress you tonight and you're going to play every second shift.' So, he put me in. He played me every second shift. I had a decent game. He raved about me in the media after the game. He just raved about me and made it so that Harry couldn't send me down. That isn't something that Glen would do. Glen would send you down and not think twice about it."

The minors were where Forbes spent the majority of his decade-long pro career. He managed to eke out 50 NHL games before he hung up his skates in 1987. "When I hung them up, I was disappointed. Anytime you have a goal of making it to the NHL, and that's what every young Canadian kid wants, and you don't make it, there's some dissatisfaction."

Eventually Mike Forbes found peace with his hockey career: "I had a real estate company for a while and you try other things in your life, but I always ended up back in a rink. That epiphany came to me when I was about 45. I said, 'What am I doing?' I was building recreational centres and ice rinks and all of a sudden I was coaching a high school team in my hometown. I thought, what's this all about? And then I found out, well, this is where I'm most comfortable."

"The place that I was most comfortable in was an ice rink. It's because of the clock. It's the only place in my world, in my entre life, where I could look to the end of the rink and see that it was 3–2. We were losing. There were five minutes left and I knew exactly what to do. No other place in my life did I have that."

Forbes has spent a lifetime in the game. He's coached college hockey at Grand Valley State University, where he won a national championship in 2011, won an IHL championship as a player, and was an assistant GM and co-owner of the Muskegon Lumberjacks and the Cleveland Lumberjacks. He was the commissioner of the Colonial Hockey League, and yes, once upon a time scored a goal that was assisted by two of the best to ever play. "Scoring a goal in the National Hockey League was nice, but really, what I took the most gratification from was that I had a lifetime in the game outside of that [goal]. In a lot of respects I was disappointed in my hockey career — but I've never been disappointed in my hockey life."

Courtesy of the Wilkes Barre Scranton Penguins

ALAIN NASREDDINE

"When I tell people this [story], I never tell them that I scored just one goal. I say I scored my first goal. It leaves room for: 'Well, maybe he scored more.'" And there is one more thing the man who served as the interim head coach of the New Jersey Devils for the majority of the 2019-20 season tells me . . .

Which we will get to in a moment. First, a little background. Nasreddine was a 31-year-old pro who had played the majority of his career in the minors, and then he found himself on the ice at Bell Centre, in his hometown of Montreal, in the dying seconds of the first period one December 2006 night. Nasreddine had been called up by the Pens from the AHL a little under two weeks earlier. "Getting up there and getting that chance, I knew at that age to just keep it simple and play my game. I had nothing to lose. It was just a bonus. I just seized my opportunity. [Penguins head coach] Mike Therrien gave me a chance. I was a defensive defenceman. I was good on the penalty kill. I had never really played on the PK in the NHL, that was my bread and butter, and

I finally got a chance and I did a good job: I was able to spend the rest of the year there."

In other words, Nasreddine was not on the Pens roster to play the role of the next Bobby Orr. Chances were, on the night of December 16, 2006, his NHL stat line would remain the same as it had in his first 30 NHL games: 0 goals, 0 assists, 0 points. "I didn't even have a point, I didn't have an assist, I didn't have a goal. At that point I just wanted an assist somewhere to get the doughnut off my stat sheet."

And as a stay-at-home defenceman just up from the minors, the chances were good that Nasreddine wouldn't be making any rushes up the ice, pinches, or charges to the net. But timing is everything: the Pens had the puck deep in the Montreal zone with the final seconds of the first period quickly ticking away; and not only did the Pens have the puck deep in the Montreal zone, the best player in the world just happened to have that puck below the goal line — it was Sidney Crosby. "I don't know what I was doing on the ice the same time as Sid. They definitely double-shifted Sid."

Nasreddine did what any reliable, stay-at-home defenceman without a single NHL goal or point would do in that situation. The clock ticking down, the Pens deep in the Montreal zone — he made a charge for the net. "I was never one to take chances offensively, but when there's very little time like that, you know they can't go back the other way and score against you. So I just figured I'd take a shot and come down the slot. Somehow Sid found me and that's how I scored my goal."

Sidney Crosby passed the puck to a streaking Alain Nasreddine and he beat Cristobal Huet in tight. The puck crossed the line with milliseconds to spare. Nasreddine's reaction was priceless. He didn't hold anything back: he raised his arms in the air, hooting and hollering as he turned and skated into the mob of his teammates. "I'm an emotional guy to start with. To this day, as well: I'm a coach, and we score a goal and I show emotion. Some coaches, they don't move. But that's not me. I still get a lot of heat about that celly. Guys say: 'Oh, did you just score the winning goal for the Stanley Cup?' I was yelling and screaming."

And here's the thing about Alain's celly: he was genuinely happy, but so were his teammates. Nasreddine was a guy who was well-known throughout the Penguins organization. He was that veteran minor league presence on the Penguins' AHL team. A lot of his then-NHL teammates were guys who once upon a time looked up to him when they were new pros in the AHL. Now he was celebrating his first NHL goal with them. "The guys were very happy. Just mentioning that gives me the goosebumps. The guys were really happy for me. I knew a lot of those guys for a while and they might have known a little bit about my situation with the doughnut on my stat sheet. And they knew I was from Montreal, and I scored in Montreal. Even Sid, when he joins the group [the celebration], you can tell he's really happy for me."

And back to that timing thing. Nasreddine's goal just beat the clock, so it came at the perfect time. The goal also came at the perfect time for Alain's brother, Samy, and a group of their friends. Alain's brother was playing in Europe at the time. The Nasreddine brothers are just a year apart, so they share a lot of friends. When Alain was on the ice at the Bell Centre, his brother, over in Europe, called their buddies who were all in an apartment in Montreal watching the game. "My brother was talking to one of our friends, and I happened to score. So my friends, they all go and jump up and down and there's screaming and yelling and celebrating, and my brother is on the other end of the phone going, 'What the hell just happened? What happened? What happened?' And the guy on the phone says: 'Your brother just scored!' My brother said, 'What? My brother scored? Stop fucking around.' 'No. He just scored! He just scored! At the Bell Centre!' Everything was just unbelievable."

The Pens went on to lose the game 6–3. Alain admits he didn't exactly have the best two periods of his life over the final 40 minutes. "We were down in the game and I still had the biggest smile on my face. I couldn't wipe it off. That cliché — gosh, I wish I could trade my goal for a win — I'm not 100 percent sure that's true in my case."

That goal is something you can never take away from Alain. It's not lost on him when he's behind the bench and he sees one of his young players find the NHL twine for the first time. "I always think some of those kids don't go through what I've gone through. Some of those kids, they score in their first 10 games in the NHL. Very rarely will you see a 30-, 32-year-old score his first goal in the NHL. You see some guys, they kind of expect it, some guys are very happy and they can't believe they just scored in the NHL. But I always go up to them and say the same thing: "No one will ever take that one away." That's kind of the feeling I have. I scored a goal and it's always going to be in the record books. It's always going to be there, so I tell those guys the same thing."

"I didn't play that many games [in the NHL], so I know how hard it was for me to play those games and make it a full season in Pittsburgh at the age of 31. So I might be a little different than some young guy who comes in at 18 or 19. Some of them might take it for granted sometimes and that's maybe the lesson I can give them."

Think about that for a second. It's true that when most first-time goal scorers snipe that first goal, they'll likely be somewhere between the ages of 20 and 25. When Alain Nasreddine scored his first NHL goal he was 31 years old and had played in over 800 games in the minors and another 30 in the NHL. He had a lengthy career and he got that goal the hard way — he earned it. Maybe that's why it stands out so much for him when he thinks back on the best moments of his pro career. "I would say it's probably at the top, if I'm going to be honest. Obviously there's my first game in the NHL, but if I had to relive each moment, I would say that goal for sure, because it was a product of commitment, dedication and just never quitting, and working. And to do it at the age I did it at, where I thought the NHL was out of reach, even though I always believed I could play, that's what I think makes it special."

And the other thing Alain told me on the phone? The chirps. From his friends, of course, who are merciless, just like my friends. "They always bust my chops. They say, 'That's how *great* Sidney Crosby is, to be able to set *you* up for a goal. That's how great Crosby is.' They like to bust my chops about that."

BRAD MORAN

For most of us, chances are your superiors don't hover over you at work, watching your every move. I would imagine that would be a little nerve-racking. But that's reality for pro hockey players, especially those looking to make the jump to the NHL: "It's a grind, mentally more than anything. You're always being watched," says Brad Moran, who had a professional career that lasted 17 seasons.

When he was 24 years old he was no different than any other American League player. He was under the microscope of scouts, doing whatever it took to get the call to the National Hockey League. Constant scrutiny in the workplace was just part of his life. "You want to make sure that you're leaving the right impression every night and that when the opportunity arises you're the guy they call. You don't know when someone is coming down or when the big club will need somebody. So, you always have to be at the top of your game."

"The best thing you can do is put it out of your mind. As soon as I would start to think about it, or you see guys thinking about it, then things would just go wrong. You have to mature quickly and you have to understand the mental part of the game. You have to just play the game and let everything else take care of itself. You can't control what someone sees or what they think of you." A cliché, maybe, but true: all a guy in the American League can do, Moran says, is "just play your game and go from there."

Whatever Moran did in late January 2004 was enough. Moran got the call from the Columbus Blue Jackets. He was going up to the NHL. He had been there before; this time, though, things were a little different. "My coach called: He was the guy who said I was going back up. I think I had been up a couple of times for one game, sent back down type of thing. This time it was a little more planned. I got to go in the day before the game. I got a couple of practices in, got in the hotel and stuff. And I got to play a home game instead of just coming in quick on the road."

For a lot of players summoned from the minors, a call-up means time on the fourth line. That was not the case for Moran on January 27, 2004. He was put on the Blue Jackets top line alongside Rick Nash, who was on his way to 41 goals that year, and David Vyborny. "It was the first time I was given an opportunity to play with some pretty skilled guys. Nash won the Rocket Richard that year [he tied for the league lead with 41 goals along with Ilya Kovalchuk and Jarome Iginla]. My role was to set guys up, and obviously you want to get that puck to the net, too."

The Blue Jackets were taking on the New Jersey Devils that night, and Moran's line was buzzing. Moran was definitely getting his chances. But he was encountering a problem, and he was by no means alone: many other NHLers had encountered this same quandary over their careers. The problem was Hall of Famer Marty Brodeur. Brodeur stopped more shots than any goalie in NHL history. (The Hall of Famer finished his career with 28,928 saves.) "I could have had three [goals] that night. I was absolutely robbed once. I was thinking, 'Am I ever going to score on this guy?'"

Moran and the Blue Jackets kept pecking away at Brodeur. In the final minute of regulation, the Blue Jackets were down 4–2. They pulled their goalie. "It was a great play by my linemates, Vyborny and Nash. Nash kind of gave me an empty net where I was actually robbed."

Brodeur had stoned Moran again. It was his third shot on goal of the night; the fourth one, milliseconds later, was the charm, "The rebound came right to me and I put it in. I figure, if you're going to score a goal you might as well score against the winningest goalie ever, so that's my claim to fame."

Moran scored with 23 seconds left in regulation. The Devils won 4–3. Moran added an assist as well for a two-point night. He was named the game's second star. Things were looking good. Two nights later, Moran was held off the scoresheet and was a minus-1 in a 6–4 loss to Nashville. And then he was sent back to the minors. The Blue Jackets had sent defenceman Darryl Sydor and a fourth-rounder to Tampa Bay for Alexander Svitov and a third-rounder. Svitov was a centre; Moran was a centre. So, that was it for Moran's stint in Columbus. "The numbers game came into effect again and I was back down."

"It's disappointing when you had a good game with some good players. You think about where it could go from there. It was frustrating and disappointing, but it was also a bit of motivation for me. I knew that I accomplished something there [in the NHL]. I made a bit of a statement. So, I was hoping that if I continued pushing . . . if Columbus didn't notice, then someone else would."

Moran never played for the Blue Jackets again. He played three more NHL games with Vancouver three years later, and he played pro right up until the end of the 2016–17 season. He spent time in Switzerland, Austria, and Sweden. He finished his professional career with a couple of years in Great Britain's Elite Ice Hockey League, where he won a championship with the Nottingham Panthers. "It's hard to put into words what it's like to win a professional championship. It's a grind. You know how bad everybody wants it, so to come out on top and win something is pretty special."

That championship came over 13 years after his one goal, against one of the greatest goalies in the history of the game. He scored on a Hall of Famer, and it was assisted by a future Hall of Famer. A pretty good story. "Like I said, it was against a Hall of Fame goalie, I'm not going to let that die."

MIKE HURLBUT

A moment in time. That's what a goal is. That's what everything is, really. It's what an injury is, too. It can and does happen in an instant. Mike Hurlbut was cruising along for the New York Rangers during the 1992–93 season. The Blueshirts were loaded with future Hall of Famers, but for some reason they were struggling in the standings. Still, Hurlbut, a 25-year-old rookie defenceman, seemed to be fitting in quite well. "The team was struggling a little bit. I went up not knowing what to expect. I just followed the advice of my old St. Lawrence University coach, Joe Marsh: just play your game and don't change. My first game was in Philly with Eric Lindros in his prime."

Hurlbut was pretty well-schooled by the time he lined up against Lindros and the Flyers. He had four years at St. Lawrence University, where he was a First-Team All-American in 1989, and he was on his second contract with Rangers. He had played out his initial three-year deal and re-signed with the Rangers in the summer of '92. "I remember like it was yesterday. One day I came back from an AHL road trip in the Maritimes. I said to my wife, 'I think I might have made a mistake re-signing with Rangers.' I had 12 points in my first 15 games and I hadn't really heard much from them. And it was literally the next day that I got called up [for the game against Philly]."

Hurlbut didn't get a point against the Flyers, but over the course of the next few games he started to fit in. He even got a little power-play time. "I was on the second power-play unit. Unfortunately I had to wait for Brian Leetch to come off after the first unit. He used to stay out for most of the two minutes, which is understandable given what a great player Brian was."

In his fifth game with Rangers, Hurlbut actually found himself on the power play with Leetch. The Rangers were pounding the Penguins. Leetch wasn't the only future Hall of Famer on the ice for New York on that PP shift. Mark Messier was on the ice. Mike Gartner was on the ice, too. That's a lot of talent. But it was Hurlbut who ended up scoring the Rangers' tenth goal of the night in an 11–3 win over the Penguins. "The goal was assisted by Leetch and Messier. A friend of mine joked afterwards that they certainly knew who to get the puck, too."

"It was a one-timer right from the blue line. At first I didn't know that I had scored because Mike Gartner was in front and he didn't miss many pucks that went near him. What a great career and a great goal scorer he was. So I wasn't even sure if I scored, initially. I just assumed he had gotten a stick on the puck." Gartner never touched the puck. The goal belonged to Mike Hurlbut. "It was five-hole from the blue line against Ken Wregget."

But maybe even better than the thrill of scoring the goal for Hurlbut was the gift that the goal was for his father. Hurlbut scored his first and only NHL goal on Ray Hurlbut's birthday. "I didn't even realize it was my dad's birthday at the time. My wife was pregnant and I was just called up. I was fulfilling a lifelong dream to play in the NHL. You kind of lose track of birthdays. He reminded me a couple of days later what a great present it was.

So, for me, that goal is a reminder of him. He passed away three years ago now."

Hurlbut added an assist in that win over the Pens, a little bonus for his father. It looked like he had finally found a way to fit in on the Rangers after a lengthy minor league apprenticeship in the organization. His timing was finally spot on, but only for a brief instant. Following his 23rd game of the season, in mid-January, Hurlbut's timing turned to bad, in an instant. During a practice drill Hurlbut collided with a teammate. He had a severely sprained MCL. His knee was blown out. He had a long recovery ahead of him. Was that injury the turning point that kept him from further developing with the Rangers?

"I think so," says Hurlburt. "If you look at it just from a statistical standpoint, how I had done in the 23 games I played for them, if you project my points out over a full season, I was doing pretty well. I was a plus. I was one of the few players on the team over those 23 games who was plus. You know things were going pretty good. But like I said, it's all part of it. I don't dwell on it whatsoever. A lot of guys in my position, they just need that opportunity to get up and establish themselves in the NHL. Sometime those opportunities present themselves and sometimes they don't. And obviously that was my big opportunity."

But it was gone. After six or seven weeks of recovery, Hurlbut was sent down to Binghamton for conditioning. The Rangers were out of the playoff race and Hurlbut finished the season in the minors. It turned that January 16, 1993, game against the Montreal Canadiens was the final one the now long-time St. Lawrence associate head coach ever played for the Rangers. "I was really excited for training camp the next year, based on how I had played in the 23 games with them. I was just loading up my car to drive down to New York for the first day of camp and I got traded to Quebec."

Hurlbut played a grand total of one NHL game for the Nordiques. He had 46 points in 77 games for the Nordiques AHL affiliate in '93–'94. The Nordiques seemed to be more interested in having a local kid in Cornwall than Hurlbut on their blue line. Hurlbut grew up 20 minutes from Cornwall, just across the border in Massena, New York. "They had moved their AHL team to Cornwall and we're trying to get some local guys to help out with the attendance. Obviously, that didn't work out. They averaged about five hundred fans a game in Cornwall. I lived at home. I drove back and forth across the border. I got to know the custom agents on both sides really well at the time."

Hurlbut's 23-game stint with the Rangers made up the bulk of the 29 career NHL games he suited up for. Yes, that injury was a turning point, but as Hurlbut says, he had his chance. He does not dwell on it. He played for 13 years as a pro. Both of his children graduated from St. Lawrence, including his son Jacob, who has a pretty strong connection to that long-ago knee injury. You see, that injury wasn't the worst thing to ever happen to Hurlbut. It happened just two days before Jacob showed up on the scene. "That made sure I was in town for his birth. The one silver lining to the injury was the fact that I was in town for Jacob's birth. I guess everything happens for a reason."

Courtesy of the Truro Bearcats

SHAWN EVANS

On November 9, 1989, Shawn Evans scored his lone NHL goal against the Quebec Nordiques in a 7–5 New York Islanders loss. It was a third-period power-play marker, which brought the Isles to within two of the Nords. Evans slid the puck past an old teammate of his, Ron Tugnutt. "Ron is an old friend of mine, and Ron and I played together with the Peterborough Petes. I won't forget that part ever. Number one — it was cool to score on Ron."

Number two? The primary assist on the goal went to future Hall of Famer Pat LaFontaine. Evans hasn't looked at his goal in years; he says it's on an old VHS tape, but he doesn't need to look at that old, grainy tape to bring back a few memories of just what a special player LaFontaine was. In fact, LaFontaine helped many a player like Evans, who was trying to establish himself in the NHL, in a very specific way. "If memory serves, there were four or five of us who moved up from Springfield that year who scored our first NHL goal. And I believe Pat set up every one of them."

Shawn Evans was on his way. He scored his first NHL goal for the team, the New York Islanders, he grew up cheering for. Little did he know there were only 10 minutes and five seconds of game time left in his NHL career. Evans scored his one goal in his ninth NHL game. It was the final game of his NHL career. Two nights later, he was a healthy scratch in Chicago. The following night, he found himself in the press box again; watching, not playing, in an NHL game. It's funny — the things that will pop up in a person's memory. For Evans it was not the score that night, not the game itself, but something most of us would likely have burned into our brains.

"I sat out a game at Madison Square Garden. I was sitting there having a hot dog, just watching the game. And then Carol Alt made her late entrance into the stands. Trust me when I say that for me, at least, the game stopped. I can tell you that. I remember that very clearly, sitting there at Madison Square, I was a healthy scratch. It wasn't long after that . . ."

It wasn't long after that he was sent down to Springfield of the American Hockey League. That memory of Carol Alt walking into the Garden is among Evans's last in the NHL. The next thing he knew, he was getting sent to the minors by Al Arbour. "Al told me how it was going to be when he called me in. You're always hoping it's not going to happen. If you don't have the blinders on, you can see it coming. He handled me with class and he handled me with honesty."

"When Mr. Arbour sent me down, he said I played very well in the two games I played. He said, 'You're on a two-way contract, I'm sending you down.' He didn't say I deserved to stay, he didn't say I did not deserve to stay, but he made the facts clear. He gave me a compliment and then he told me the cold reality of how the business works." When you're on a two-way contract, chances are you're the easiest guy to send to the farm. You don't have to clear waivers. If it was a numbers game, Evans was caught up in it. Goal or no goal, his time in the NHL was finished.

Now approaching close to 20 years as the head coach of the Junior A Truro Bearcats of the Maritime Hockey League, Evans doesn't talk too much about his lone NHL goal. He doesn't mention it to his players. But he is reminded of that goal every time he goes to the fridge. "The Islanders did a nice job. They put the puck on a plaque for me. It's moved around in my home over the years. Now it sits in the kitchen. That's where my wife put it. I see the puck regularly. My daughters are 13 and 11, so it comes up with them once in a while. But it's not something that I talk about here in the small community that I live in."

A little over three decades ago, Evans was a high-scoring defenceman with the Peterborough Petes of the Ontario Hockey League. A second-round pick of the New Jersey Devils in the 1983 Draft, Evans racked up seasons of 48, 108, and 99 points on the Petes blue line. Five years after leaving the Petes, he beat his old Peterborough teammate at the Quebec Colisée for his first NHL goal. A few days after that he was sent back to the AHL, but still, he had faith he'd get another shot: "You always hope [to return to the NHL]; [hoping] is what an American Hockey Leaguer does. Speaking for myself, I sure did."

Evans kept hoping, but that call never came. He played on a Springfield club that won the Calder Cup in 1989–90. Just a few months after scoring his first NHL goal, Evans put up 17 points in 18 playoff games and was a Calder Cup champ. But the following season, the call never came. That's when the reality of his situation began to sink in. "As a professional minor-leaguer you always have to take a deep breath when the realization comes that your day is up, that your NHL dream is over. Then it's time to move on: What's the best I can do? As a very proud American Hockey League player, what are my best options from here? You always hope [for a call up], but then reality sets in and you can reset your goals."

And that is when adult decisions have to be made in what was once a kid's game. You start to understand that your one NHL goal is going to be your only NHL goal. In the early 1990s, reality for steady minor-leaguers usually meant one thing: it was time to move on and make some money, either in Europe or the International League. Evans started with a brief cameo in Switzerland during the '90-'91 season, and then in the fall of 1992 he went to the "I." He signed with the Milwaukee Admirals. He continued to score. He was nearly a point-a-game player — 78 points in 79 games. He spent parts of five of his final seven professional seasons in the International League. "The IHL was great. You had the Las Vegas stop, Long Beach, and San Francisco was in the league. For us veteran players it was a good hockey league. There were a lot of former NHL guys. It was a proud league to play in."

Shawn Evans wrapped up his pro career with the Mohawk Valley Prowlers of the United League during the 1998–99 season. His head coach was Dave "The Hammer" Schultz. Evans played for countless coaches during his career, and he had countless teammates. He lists Al Arbour, Jim Roberts, and Bruce Boudreau among his favourite coaches to play for. And it's the people we talk about during our chat, more so than his only NHL goal.

"It really is the people. It comes right down to the basics. Hockey players, when they meet somebody, they *always* shake hands. In regular life, there are many people who do not. Hockey teaches you respect. And it's the people I met in hockey who taught me the little things about hockey and how to represent yourself. Those are lessons I take forever."

When you score your first NHL goal, you think there are more to come. And a lot of people thought plenty of NHL goals would be on the way for the kid who led all OHL defenceman in scoring, with 109 points in 1983–84. Those 109 points are still the sixth-most ever put up by a blueliner in a single OHL campaign.

"Was I at peace? That's a good question. Well . . . when it's over, it's over. For me it was. You always thought that you could do a little bit better, that's how I feel. How would I put it to you? I'm usually a blunt guy. I was drafted high. My statistics and the individual success I had in Peterborough, I'm very, very, proud of it. I do know that I still hold most of the defenceman records. The game has changed; it's going to be hard to beat some of those numbers that I put up."

"I was a guy with some off-ice issues, I had a bad time. The only regret I have is that I'll never know, without those off-ice issues, if I could have done a little bit better. That, I'll never know. I made peace with that a long time ago."

What specifically were those off-ice issues? Evans chooses not to get into the details, but he does get to the point: "I'm not going to quite say it to you, but sometimes you get sidetracked. And I got sidetracked for a little while. By the time I put it all together, I kind of felt it was too late. I was an offensive player. I certainly was no Don Awrey in my own end. There's always a question out there for me that I'll never know the answer to. But I'm at peace with my career and I'm very proud of what I got to accomplish."

DAN LUCAS

Dan Lucas and Wayne Gretzky /
Courtesy of the Sault Ste. Marie Greyhounds

For most NHLers, it's a really long road to the NHL. For others, it's a really long drive. Dan Lucas started his drive from the campus of the University of British Columbia and ended up in Philadelphia, with a one-year pit stop in Sault Ste. Marie, Ontario, in between. Lucas's cross-continent adventure began months before he stepped behind the wheel, when the WCHL's Victoria Cougars traded him to the Edmonton Oil Kings in 1976: "I got traded for a new car and $20,000 for five players." That was at Christmas. Lucas had no intention of leaving BC. He was, by major-junior standards of the time, a scholarly type. "I was one of two guys on the team who went to high school." He was in his senior year and wanted to graduate.

So, Lucas didn't go to Edmonton. The following season, he still refused to move from BC. He enrolled at the University of British Columbia. He was the youngest player on the Thunderbirds but still finished second in team scoring with 28 points in 24 games. He was one and done at UBC. "The next year came up. It was my draft year and teams started bugging me again. 'What are you going to do?'"

Lucas started taking calls from all over the junior hockey landscape. One of them was from a man named Muzz MacPherson. Earlier in his junior days, Lucas and his Saskatchewan Junior A champion Humboldt Broncos squad faced off against MacPherson's Manitoba champion Portage Terriers in the Anavet Cup Final. Evidently, Lucas made an impression. A few years later, MacPherson was in charge of the Sault Ste. Marie Greyhounds. MacPherson made his pitch: "He says, 'I got this kid. He was our number-one pick in the [OHA] draft. He's unbelievable. I think you could play with him. I think you guys would really complement each other.'"

Lucas was sold. He hopped in his car and took off: "I had relatives, so I spent an overnight in Winnipeg and then I drove from Winnipeg straight to the Soo."

When he arrived in Sault Ste. Marie, the 19-year-old Lucas was introduced to that 16-year-old kid that Muzz MacPherson had told him about on the phone. "I got out of the car and walked in and Muzz introduced me to . . . Wayne Gretzky."

"He was a kid. I was probably not as in tune to his reputation as everybody in Ontario, because the kid was burning it up, obviously." But when Dan Lucas locked eyes with Gretzky, a light bulb went off: "I looked right at him and I said, 'Were you on the cover of the *Star Weekly*?' When I was a kid in British Columbia I saw it. He said, 'Yeah.' He was on the cover of the *Star Weekly* when he was 10 or 11 years old or something. I thought, 'This is that kid.'"

Lucas had just driven more than halfway across Canada, and he was understandably a little sluggish, but after a couple of days, he began to see the magic that Wayne Gretzky could make on the ice. "After a couple of days I got my legs and we started getting into it. I played with him right away. He was a good kid. I liked him a lot."

Playing on a line with "The Great One," Dan Lucas finished second on the Greyhounds with 50 goals and 117 points. You can probably guess who was first. That spring, Lucas went 14th overall in the NHL Draft. When training camp approached, Lucas began his drive again. He got behind the wheel of his Ford Cortina and headed for the Flyers training camp. A few short weeks later, he was on the ice at the Spectrum for his fourth NHL game. His Flyers were taking on the Pittsburgh Penguins. The reality of making it all the way to the NHL was still amazing: "Greg Millen, who I played with in Sault Ste. Marie, was the backup goalie for Pittsburgh. Before the game, we kind of gave each other a little chuckle. We were sort of pinching ourselves, like 'This is the life. We're in the *the* Apple,' type of thing. This is the big time."

Later that night, late in the third period, Lucas beat Millen's Pittsburgh partner, Denis Herron, for his first NHL goal. "It's like it happened yesterday . . . I played on the right side, so I was on the off-wing. It was almost like a two-on-one, and Bill Barber made a cross-ice pass. It was a one-timer. We ended up winning the game 3–1. That was pretty cool."

The other assist on Lucas's goal went to his old Victoria junior teammate Mel Bridgman. His buddy Millsy was on the bench for the Penguins. Lucas was named third star of the night in just his fourth NHL game. This was easy stuff, right? "No," laughs Lucas. "I think a lot of guys get rattled a little bit if you come from juniors and you're playing and you're getting lots of ice time, and you're in all kinds of situations. But when you get in the NHL, there's a pecking order right away. You have to go back to ground zero and you've got to earn your way."

That philosophy was hammered down by the Flyers brass just a few days later. Once again it was time for Lucas to hop back into the Ford Cortina. He was ordered by the Flyers to hit the road and join the Maine Mariners of the American Hockey League. First stop: Springfield, Massachusetts. "After practice one morning, they said, 'You're going to play for the Mariners. They're playing in Springfield tonight. Here's the road map on how to get there.'"

"I think I was pretty hard on myself. I wasn't shocked, but I could have had more of a little get-go attitude when I first got there. It was like starting all over again," Lucas says. He was not alone: many players do not enjoy that first taste of pro hockey reality. "When I got there, I only had six or seven goals up until Christmas, but by the end of the year, I ended up with 21 goals. So I got my act together in the second half and I figured out [what to do] if I wanted back up there."

Lucas spent the rest of the season in Portland; in fact, he ended up winning a Calder Cup. His Mariners swept the New Haven Nighthawks and won the Cup in the fourth game of the series. But they didn't win it in Portland. And they didn't win it in New Haven either. This is classic '70s minor league hockey stuff. "It was funny, we ended up winning the Calder Cup in the Springfield rink — the place where I had my first game when the Flyers sent me down. We were supposed to play in New Haven, but they had something going on at their rink, so they moved that game to Springfield."

"If the AHL had a barn, Springfield [arena] was it. Lots of history, and a lot of great hockey players went through Springfield, but that rink was about the closest thing you'd find to some of those older buildings in Canada."

Dan Lucas never made it back to the NHL. He played the next season in Maine as well. In October 1980, he signed a free agent deal with the Colorado Rockies. A few months later, Lucas was finished. In what may seem crazy to all us hockey wannabes, Dan Lucas made the decision, after just three seasons of pro hockey, to retire. "There were probably half a dozen guys on the team in Maine that were married with kids, and I figured if I couldn't get back up to play in the NHL after three years, I just figured I didn't want to be playing hockey — riding a bus in the minors. I was going to make a change in my life."

Lucas was done. He met his future wife while playing with the Mariners, and that's where he decided to start his new life, in Maine. He was only 23. "I don't think I really struggled," Lucas says of his life right after hockey. He went back to school and finished his degree in business administration. Lucas has owned his own real estate company for over 30 years. "I wanted to create my own business. People in my family back home were like, 'Are you crazy? Real estate? You don't know anybody.' But I said, 'You know what, you just gotta put one foot in front of the other and build relationships.'"

But still, a hockey wannabe like myself needed to know; so, I asked him: "Do you regret walking away from the game at such a young age?"

"I think there's always that twinge, you know — could you have given it a better shot to get back up there? But in the greater scheme of life of where I was and where I'm at now, there's no question I made the right decision when I made it."

CHAPTER THREE
JUST IN TIME

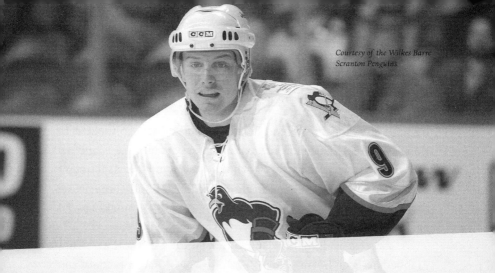

*Courtesy of the Wilkes Barre
Scranton Penguins*

CONNOR JAMES

Every beer-leaguer on the planet has been there. Your game starts at 7 p.m., but you're running late. Maybe you're stuck in traffic. Maybe your boss made you work late. Maybe your kids just wouldn't let you get out of the house. Connor James was stuck in traffic. "It was all stop and go. Stop and go."

The difference between you and Connor James is that you were running late for beer league; he was trying to get to a game at Nassau Coliseum. It was the Penguins against the Islanders on February 26, 2008. The day started normally enough. James was having a ho-hum day in Wilkes-Barre, Pennsylvania, the home of the Penguins AHL affiliate. With nothing better to do, he decided to run out and buy a few groceries: "I was shopping and my name got called over the intercom speaker calling me to reception. I thought I had lost my keys or my wallet or something. So I walked over there and my head coach, Todd Richards, was on the phone."

It was trade deadline day. Maybe Richards was going to tell Connor that the Pens moved him in a deal. No, that wasn't it. But it was still big news. The Pens pulled off a blockbuster deal. They sent Colby Armstrong, two other players, and a first-rounder to Atlanta for Marian Hossa and Pascal Dupuis. The problem was, there was no way Hossa and Dupuis would be able to make it to Long Island for that night's Penguins game against the Islanders. And that was why Richards was calling. James and his AHL team-mate Nathan Smith were getting called up for the game. Now they just had to make their way to Long Island: "I quickly raced back to our rink and grabbed my stuff."

A car was waiting for James and Smith. As soon as James grabbed his gear, he jumped in. The only thing that stood between James and the NHL was about 250 kilometres and New York rush hour traffic. The driver didn't seem to be in that big of a hurry, says James: "He was just taking his time."

As the drive went on, one thing became very clear to James, who already had seven games played on his NHL resumé. He was not going to make it for the opening faceoff. "We're late, late, late. The game starts and we're still in the car. We're sitting in the car listening to the first period of the game on the radio."

James, Smith, and their driver were crawling through traffic. There was nothing anyone could do but wait, drive, and wait. The car finally arrived at the arena. James thought he was in for a leisurely night in the press box, though; after all, the first period was already over. Wrong. Pens Coach Michel Therrien greeted James and Smith when they arrived. "He said, 'You guys are still playing. So, warm up.' We quickly went on the bike for about five minutes."

By the time James was all geared up and all warmed up, the second period had started. Just like a late-running beer-leaguer, James had to wait for a whistle to join his team. "We skated out after a whistle midway through the second period."

The rest of the second period went off without a hitch and James headed back to the Pens room with his team up 2–1. "Between the second and third, Georges Laraque was sitting there joking around with Nathan Smith and I. He was like, 'I guess if one of you scores, you'll get to stay up.'" Laraque was right, kind of.

Late in the third with the Pens up 3–1, Connor James found himself on the power play. He's not really sure why. "I don't know what I was doing out there. It was kind of a weird goal, too. It was a two-on-one, and the guy I was with was Ryan Whitney and he was a defenceman. He passed it over to me and I scored. I have the puck. That's pretty much it. The trainer took the puck and put a little piece of tape around it."

When the clock ticked down to end the third, that wasn't quite the end of a long day for Connor James. He had scored, but Laraque was not correct. James was sent back to the farm anyway. The Pens had to make room for Hossa and Dupuis on the roster. James hopped in a car and it was back to Wilkes-Barre. The Pens' latest additions would be in Pittsburgh's lineup for the next game. James did get the call back to Pittsburgh shortly thereafter, though. Connor James' NHL career consisted of 16 games, one goal, and one very long commute to work. "I just remember, joking in the car, going, 'This is a waste of time. We're not going to make it. We might as well just turn around.'"

But they didn't. They just kept on driving and made it to the rink in time for Connor James to score his only NHL goal. "When Therrien said, 'You guys are still playing,' we went, 'Holy shit! Okay!'"

It was a pretty good decision by the coach.

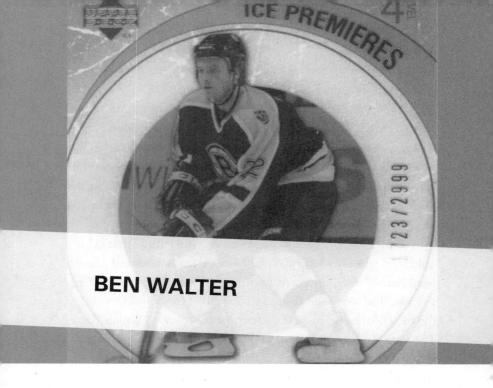

ICE PREMIERES

123/2999

BEN WALTER

"I remember thinking, 'This is going to be a good story someday, but right now, it's not.'" That's what went through Ben Walter's mind when he walked into the New York Islanders dressing room just a few minutes before the opening faceoff of a game against the Tampa Bay Lightning on March 11, 2008. What he didn't know is that his story was going to have a much better end than the then–23-year-old could have ever imagined.

It all started the night before. Walter has a few people to thank for the story of his first NHL goal. First off, let's start with "The Boss," Bruce Springsteen. Ben Walter was playing for the Islanders AHL affiliate in Bridgeport, Connecticut, during his third pro season. His mom, Jenn, was in Bridgeport visiting Ben. On the final night of her trip, Ben decided to give his mother, a Bruce Springsteen superfan, a little treat. The Boss was playing at Nassau Coliseum, the home of the New York Islanders. Walter made a few calls, and voila: he got a spot for himself and his mom in the Islanders suite at the Bruce Springsteen concert. They made the drive to Long Island and took in the show.

"It was a good concert. We had fun. Mom was flying out the next morning. After the concert, I drove her to the airport hotel and then I drove back to Bridgeport. We had a practice the next day. I got home pretty late, but it was a special time for Mom. I got up for practice. It was one of those ones where I had to just get through it and then go home and have a nap."

Ben Walter did make it through that morning practice, but a nap was not in the cards. Sleep was the last thing he would be doing on this day. At around the same time Walter was on the ice in Bridgeport, one of the New York Islanders centres was injured during the morning skate in Tampa for that night's game against the Lightning. The call went out to Bridgeport. The Islanders needed a player for that night's game just over 1900 kilometres south in Tampa. "I got off the ice and they told me I was getting called up. Obviously you're always excited. It's a good opportunity. You forget how tired you are, you just decide you'll figure everything out and you'll get a nap on the plane and it'll be fine. Now usually in my experience when I got called up before that, the team would set up a car to get you, it is pretty set up for you, but this time they told me they were scrambling and I had to get to LaGuardia Airport as soon as I could."

The adventure began. Walter went home, grabbed his passport and some clothes, and started the drive back to New York, where he had been the night before, watching The Boss with his mother: "I jumped in my car and just drove. You know it's not the easiest thing driving through New York to LaGuardia. I ended up making it on time for the flight. I don't even remember where I parked my car. I was just running into the airport with my bag and my suitcase."

Walter was on time. His flight was not. In fact it was delayed a few times. Eventually the plane took off and he arrived in Tampa around 5:45 — game time was 7:00. Once Walter grabbed his gear he had another problem. The car that was supposed to pick him up and drive him to the arena was long gone. The driver got tired of waiting for the delayed flight to arrive and took off. "I ran out to get a cab. I had been sweating the whole time. I get in the cab. I had never been to Tampa before. The driver asked me, 'Where are you going?' I told him I was going to the arena. He said, 'Okay.' He casually drove to the arena. It was 6:15, then 6:20. I was looking at my watch, thinking, 'Warm-up is going on right now. I'm going to miss warm-up.' He pulled up to the rink. He didn't really know where to go. I figured that the players' entrance had to be around the back somewhere. We eventually got to the right spot, and I got out of the cab with all my stuff."

Time was ticking. Walter was in a hurry, but as soon as he turned around to walk into the arena, he was caught under the lights. "I had never had this before. You know how on Sportsnet, they always do it, especially in the playoffs, where they show the players walking into the arena, and Don Cherry is talking about the suits and how good the guys look, and that sort of thing. I never had that before. But when I got out of the cab, a TV camera was there waiting for me. I started walking into the arena and the camera [man] was in front of me, walking backwards, recording me going into the arena. I had my gear and my suitcase and I was thinking, 'Well, that's something to remember later. I'm at least maybe going to make it on the pre-game show.'"

Once his Hollywood moment was over, Walter hunted down the Islanders dressing room. The Isles warm-up was finished. The players were sitting there, waiting for the opening faceoff and waiting for the final piece of that night's lineup to arrive. That's when Walter thought, 'This is going to be a good story': "I just stroll in and the boys just start dying laughing. They thought it was the funniest thing. We had a good group, a lot of good guys. They understood [my plight]. A lot of guys on the team had been in the minors with me. It was funny to them, but for me, I was 23, pretty young still. It was just crazy."

Walter got dressed and then took the advice of his head coach Ted Nolan and took a few laps to stretch things out. Then he sat. And sat. The Islanders got into penalty trouble and Walter got the call. All of a sudden, Walter was on the PK against a very stacked Tampa power play. "And that was when Tampa had St. Louis and Lecavalier. They had a pretty good team. It was my first shift. My legs were just done. I had no warm-up, nothing. They didn't score on the power play, which was good."

Walter survived that lethal Tampa PP, but the rest of the game wasn't exactly a Picasso for his side. Midway through the third the Islanders were down 5–2. Walter got the call again — this time he got a chance on the power play. "Nolan put me out. I won a draw. There was a quick shot from the point and I got a stick on it. That was it. It was one of those things where you get back to the bench and the guys were all giving me high-fives. They were all happy for me. It was nice for me because the guys knew what kind of a day it had been for me, what the life of a minor league player was like."

When the final buzzer went, the Islanders left the ice with an 8–4 loss. One of their players was particularly bagged, even though he only had 6:31 of ice time: "I was exhausted. I remember getting on the team bus after the game and just sitting there, thinking, 'I'm glad this day is done.' Looking back now, I'm so happy it happened. I could have completely missed the game, really. Getting there on time was enough."

The Islanders did Walter a solid and kept him around for the next game in Florida and a road trip to Montreal, where his dad, Ryan, had skated for the Canadiens for so many years. "I got to stay on the road trip for a bit, that was fun. I think they probably felt they [owed me]. After the game in Florida, we didn't play for three or four days, but we went right to Montreal. They probably could have sent me down and brought me back up for the game in Montreal, but they let me stay with the team."

After the game against the Canadiens, Ben Walter was sent back down to Bridgeport. His mom felt a little guilty about the whole thing; she thought her son wouldn't have been so tired if he hadn't taken her to see The Boss the night before that game. In her defence, she had no idea her son would be called up. And as Ben says, he got a pretty good story out of the whole adventure. And he is reminded of his goal every time he hears The Boss. "I hear him all the time whenever we're at my parents' house. Mom always has him on. And when I hear him, that's the memory, just being at the concert and the whole next day."

"Mom always tells the story about how she felt bad keeping me up that late and going to a concert the night before I got called up. And then she finishes with, 'But he scored his first goal . . . so I think I did something right.'"

CHAPTER FOUR

FAMILY TIES

DAVE HANSON

He may have only scored a single goal in the NHL, but to a lot of hockey fans, Dave Hanson is royalty. He sure as hell is to me. He's a legend, even though some of his fans may not know that he played the game as a pro. "We get asked a lot, 'Hey, did you guys really play hockey?'"

The answer is yes. Dave Hanson played hockey — a lot of hockey. But the long-time minor-leaguer and NHLer who had stints with Detroit and Minnesota is better known to most of North America, and to the world for that matter, not as a former pro player, but as one of the Hanson Brothers from the greatest movie of all time: *Slap Shot*. "It doesn't cease to amaze me at all, especially the longevity of it. I mean, the film came out in 1977; I retired in 1984, and it was probably close to 1990 or '91 when suddenly, a fluke thing, the three of us [Dave, and Steve and Jeff Carlson] got back together and suddenly this thing just started snowballing."

The *Slap Shot* snowball just continues to get bigger and bigger. Dave picked up the phone to talk to me just a couple of nights after he and the boys made an appearance at a Minnesota Wild game, followed by an appearance in Fort Wayne, Indiana. Hanson's been hearing the lines from *Slap Shot* for over 40 years now. From fans and from players, who are, let's face it, often fans themselves. "When the movie came out, the fun part was the players coming up to you on a faceoff and throwing lines at you from the movie. Then they would laugh. And then later, you're out there throwing haymakers at each other."

The movie came out in 1977. Dave Hanson hit the back of an NHL net three years later, in between haymakers and chuckles, on a February 1980 night for the Minnesota North Stars, in a game against his first NHL team, in Detroit. "It was the first year that the Joe was opened. I had played in the old Olympia prior to that. I remember coming into the building and thinking, 'Oh my gosh! What a huge cavern.' It was all concrete. A little different to the kind of rinks we were used to playing in."

The North Stars were the latest stop for Hanson's vagabond hockey career. It included stops in places like Johnstown, Rhode Island, Kansas City, Detroit, and Birmingham. Before the North Stars picked him up in a trade with the Wings for futures on January 3, 1980, Hanson was on loan, playing with Birmingham in the Central League. In Birmingham, Hanson was playing for the same coach he played for with Birmingham's WHA entry the previous two seasons — the legendary John Brophy. Brophy was old school, tough as nails. He was Dave Hanson's kind of guy: "I got to understand John and was able to play regularly for him. Seriously, it got to the point that when he moved on to other teams, he wanted to take me with him. When he went to Nova Scotia, I said, 'John, please, I don't want to go to Nova Scotia. Leave me alone.'"

Let me interrupt here for a personal note. I find this information annoying, because it means I could have seen Dave Hanson play, live and in the flesh, when I was a kid. The Nova Scotia Voyageurs played just 90 minutes from my hometown of Pictou.

Brophy was their head coach from the fall of 1981 until the spring of 1984. Bummer. "I just said to Broph, I'd been to Nova Scotia a couple of times and whenever I'd gone up there the friggin' snowbanks were 50 feet high and it was freezing cold. But I loved him. I loved the man. I loved playing for him. Even after we went in different directions, we stayed very close."

The good news? When Hanson was sent to the North Stars, he didn't have to change a thing. His new coach in Minnesota, Glen Sonmor, was as close to Brophy as you could get. "Of all the coaches I played for, and I had quite a few in my professional career, Glen and Broph were my two favourites. They were basically the same person. They made it pretty simple. The rules were clear: they wanted an honest effort 100 percent of the time. They wanted hard work. And don't shy away from the tough part of the game, and be loyal to your coach and your teammates."

Hanson started off his 12th game with the North Stars the usual way. He dropped the gloves with Mike Foligno at 7:53 of the first period. "I don't recall much of the fight. Mike was a big tough guy. I played with him a little bit in Adirondack. But I don't really recall any specific details of our run-in together."

Pretty routine stuff, but then in the third, Hanson scored NHL goal number one. It came late in the game in a 7–5 Detroit win. "I was on a line with Mike Polich and Tommy Younghans. We were kind of like the third, maybe even the fourth grinder line. I remember simply being out there grinding away and getting a pass. I was in the slot. I rifled a wrist shot and it went between the legs of Rogie Vachon. Whenever I see Rogie, I'll kid him — I tell people that at least I scored on a Hall of Famer with my one goal. I saved it for that."

"Glen presented me the puck after the game and congratulated me. Then he sort of said, 'Just don't start thinking you're a goal scorer.'"

"I think anybody's first goal in the National Hockey League is pretty spectacular and memorable and certainly it was for the player I was. It was pretty cool. And to score it against the team that had signed me and moved me along and traded me to Birmingham . . . I have to admit, it was a little extra sweet. It was great, but yet unfortunate that it was the only goal that I would ever score in the NHL. I'm very happy I got at least one. At least it gave my son a goal to shoot for. Maybe he could beat his old man."

Now fast-forward about 29 years. Dave Hanson was now not only a former pro, a Hanson brother, and a former hockey executive, he was also something else — he was an NHL dad. His son Christian was a rookie with the Toronto Maple Leafs.

In his third NHL game, Christian Hanson scored his first NHL goal. And it was on a Hall of Famer, too. Christian Hanson found the net on his boyhood idol, Martin Brodeur. Christian first met Brodeur when he was a kid and tagged along to a charity game with Dave. "Marty was there and got a picture with Christian and from that point on Marty was Christian's hero and idol and Christian wanted to be a goalie. And then to score his first goal against Marty — it was obviously very thrilling. And for me, I was probably more thrilled. The funny part about it was, afterwards, Christian called me up and he said, 'Hey, Dad, do you think I should ask Marty to sign the puck?' I said, 'Yeah, go for it.'"

A trainer took the puck to Martin Brodeur in the Devils room. He asked Brodeur to sign it. "Marty said, 'Yeah . . . I'd love to do it, but I don't think [I can]. Lou [Lamoriello]'s in the room. I don't think Lou would appreciate it, because we lost. I don't think he'd appreciate me signing a puck from a goal that was scored against us in a loss.' So, it never happened."

Dave Hanson was now simply a hockey dad. When the cameras cut to him in the stands you could see that look of contentment on his face, like any other dad watching their son play — and score — in the NHL. "Like any dad, I took my little son out onto the rink and started the skating part. And when he got to the age of being able to play some organized hockey I started coaching him from that point on. I coached him up until he was about

16 years old. I'll be honest with you, I never had aspirations for him; and some parents do live through their kids, but I never had dreams of him playing in the National Hockey League. I was just having a blast coaching him and being with him on road trips. I was enjoying that journey. And as he continued to move along and got into junior hockey, I was saying what a great experience — I get to continue watching my kid play hockey. He's a good hockey player and he loves the game as much as I do. As far as I was concerned, the icing on the cake was when he got a full ride to Notre Dame."

Christian, just like his father, was never drafted, but right after his college career came to an end, the NHL came calling — and Dave was there to answer the call. "His senior year they got upset in the regionals, and on the ride back from Grand Rapids, Burkie [Brian Burke, the Leafs GM at the time] calls me on the phone. And says, 'Hey Dave, we want to sign Christian.' And that was just jubilation."

The Leafs signed Christian Hanson on March 31st, 2009. One week later, he scored that goal against the Devils to join his old man as an NHL goal scorer. He finished his career on top of the family standings with three career goals. Dad watched every second of it. "It was just fun. It was a fun ride. I enjoyed it all the way."

I'd give almost anything to score a goal in the NHL. But for most players, it's just a part of the journey, if they're lucky enough to make it to the NHL. Now, imagine if your journey included being coached by Herb Brooks at the University of Minnesota; and your journey included a role beside Paul Newman in the greatest sports movie of all time; and your journey included watching your son score an NHL goal.

Dave tells me, during our call: "When you're in the minors, you are working your tail off because the objective was, at that time, to get to the WHA or the NHL. But to get there and be a part of it exceeded any expectations that I ever had of my life as a professional athlete. And then to score a goal in the NHL, I kind of had the mentality of 'Hey, even the blind squirrel finds a nut every once in a while.' But to be a part of that league, that team, those guys, and that level of how a pro athlete is treated and revered — that was the fun part of that journey, more than the goal."

RICHIE REGEHR

A little over half an hour after Richie Regehr scored his first NHL goal, he was pulled aside for a between-periods interview on the Calgary Flames broadcast. Regehr put on his best "I'm-not-all-that-excited" face and got ready to answer a few questions from Flames broadcaster Mark Stiles. "In those days, you sort of stuck to your thing. You tried to reword the question in your answer. Because I was so excited, I was just sort of reverting to what I had been taught in media relations. It was, 'Yeah, I'm excited, we still have a game.' All that stuff."

In other words, despite the pure adrenalin rush he was still undergoing just 30 minutes after his first goal, Richie Regehr was not going to give Stiles anything: just spit out clichés and try to look like a veteran NHLer. This is how the interview began.

Mark Stiles: "Richie, you get your first goal tonight, we're going to have a look at it on the monitor. Tell us about this first one ever in the National Hockey League."

Richie: "All right, I thought I got the puck from Lombo there, the guy was right on me, I didn't think I had much time, so I just tried to get it to the net. And, uh, that's Chuckie there who did a great job of screening. That's all there is to it, I guess."

Once the camera cuts back to Regehr after the goal was shown, he is not showing much emotion at all. He has half a smirk, and you can kind of tell he's trying not to look too happy about scoring his first NHL goal. What did he really want to say during that interview? This is what he admits he really wanted to say all these years later: "It's awesome. I love it. I couldn't wait for it. I'm glad I actually scored and got it over with!"

That Regehr goal likely wouldn't have even made the highlight reels if it wasn't his first NHL goal — it was nothing spectacular. Just a nice little seeing-eye shot from the blue line, a wrister that beat Dan Cloutier low blocker side. It gave the Flames a 2–0 lead en route to a 5–3 win over the Kings. It may not have been the flashiest goal ever scored in NHL history, but it was enough for Regehr: "At that point, I was just excited to play [in the NHL]. I was being called up and sent down a lot. It was on the power play. I think that was one of my first chances to play the power play. At that point I was a big power-play guy in the American League, so I was used to it, but I never got the chance in the NHL. Yes, I was excited!"

It was Richie Regehr's first NHL tally, but unlike a lot of first-time NHL goal scorers, he had felt that feeling before. He had scored an NHL goal before, albeit temporarily. "I played in my first NHL game and I actually scored," Richie says with a laugh.

That game was on December 29, 2005, just under a year before he scored his first real NHL goal. Do you follow? Regehr scored his first NHL goal one year before he scored his first NHL goal. The "first" one only lasted for a couple of hours. "After the game, they went back and took it away from me. They gave it to Steve Reinprecht. It was a game-winning goal. Everyone was like, 'Yeah, your first game, your first goal.' I said, 'Yeah, awesome.'

But then they reviewed it and they changed it. I said, 'I don't care. I still got a game-winning assist.' The guys were all bugging me the next day."

On the bright side, Regehr never was presented with the puck from that "first" goal, so he never had to give it back. That would have been awkward. As for getting your first NHL goal taken away, Regehr, like he said, was just happy his team got the win. "I think he tipped it, so I wasn't going to say anything. I think I looked back on it and tried to find the replay, thinking, 'Did he really tip it?' But I didn't really care. I ended up getting one on my own."

It took almost a year, but when Richie did get his very own, official first NHL goal, it was all the more special because his brother was there to see it. And he wasn't only there to see it, he was also wearing a Flames jersey. It wasn't one of those souvenir knock-off jerseys. Robyn Regehr was wearing No. 28 for the Flames that night; the older of the Regehr brothers was also a Flames defenceman. "It was awesome. I still remember the first couple of times in training camp in Calgary, when we got the lineup, and we said, 'Oh, we're practising together.' My dad drove through the night just to watch us practise, because we were skating together. It was not a short trip. Rosthern was about six and a half hours away. He was a crazy hockey dad in that regard. He would just drive to Calgary for the games, drive back, and work the next day."

"We didn't get to play with each other a ton during the regular season just because Robyn was one of the top shutdown guys. I was used sparingly. We were two different types of players, but we did play together in the exhibition season."

"In Edmonton once, a bigger guy rammed me across the ice and I sort of just side-stepped him, being a smaller guy. I went skating up the ice, and out of my peripheral vision I could see Robyn taking off after him behind me. That's the brotherly bond right there. It was awesome just to experience playing with my brother. Rather than saying 'I have a brother in the NHL,' I got to play with my brother [in the NHL]."

Robyn and Richie never said much after Richie's first goal; they didn't really have to. They only got the chance to play one more game together. It was a week later. That night against the Vancouver Canucks, Richie suffered a concussion. He didn't play for the Flames again for the rest of the season, and it was his final NHL game. That summer Richie had a decision to make about his hockey life. He was an up-and-down player in the NHL. He was going through some injuries. He chose to go to Europe and signed a deal with the Frankfurt Lions in Germany.

"I had a few concussions. It made my decision, not easy . . . but a lot more straightforward. I wanted to continue to play hockey. I wanted to give myself the best chance to make a career of this. I knew the next hit could be the last. [Europe had] fewer games, the bigger ice, not as physical, not as big. What I learned is, it's just a lot more laid back there than the NHL."

But Richie didn't plan on staying in Europe for the long term. When most North American pros head to Europe, it is for good. Richie hoped to come back. Unlike a lot of North Americans who keep that dream alive, his dream could have come true. "Not many people know this story," he tells me. "After my second year, Darryl Sutter, he always told me, 'You get better, you'll be back here, you'll be back here.' So, after my second year in Europe, he actually offered me a one-way contract with Calgary."

That's the dream for any North American playing in Europe. Richie Regehr turned it down. That may sound crazy to you and me. That may sound crazy to a lot of North Americans playing in Europe. But that's what Richie Regehr did when he was 26 years old and still had a lot of hockey left in him: "I thought I would continue to have a great career in Europe. I thought coming back, being that players were bigger, stronger, faster, and the smaller ice — I wanted to have a life after hockey. It wasn't 'I'm an NHL player, I have to have that.' I played [in the NHL]. I tried. I don't really need that in my life. I'd rather have a good life after hockey and play hockey."

It was the fact that Richie already had a taste of the big league that made the decision to turn down the offer easier. He admits that if he had never played an NHL game at that point, he would have signed Sutter's offer right away. "Oh yeah, for sure. No question about that. It's still awesome thinking back on every time I got called up. You'd get that call, you'd be like, 'Holy shit. This is awesome.' Your first time you're on a charter plane, you think, 'This is awesome.' It is the place to play. You get anything you want and everything you want. You're the one. That's the pinnacle for any hockey player — to play in the NHL."

But Richie said no to a second chance at life in the NHL. He said no to a chance to score another goal in the NHL. But he has no regrets: "None at all."

Regehr played in Europe until the 2017–18 season. He spent all but three of his European seasons in Germany. He was a league champ five times. "Championships are just unbelievable. The party after, the elation, the feeling that you won your last game. They are two different feelings: that NHL goal is awesome just because it sort of relates to what I said, the NHL is the NHL — the best league in the world. The goal is more of a right-now-right-here feeling. A championship is more you're going to feel it for a longer time. You'll look back and you'll remember all the stuff that went into that."

"The goal is still great and I appreciate it. I love it. I still see the little plaque with the puck and the picture, but the championships are just totally different. It's hard to relate to both of them in the same aspect."

"I remember something from every year, whether it be the championships or what I learned or what I was put through, different injuries, different positions, things to have moulded me into what I am now."

Regehr is a hockey coach and skills development instructor in Saskatoon — a hockey lifer. He's a guy who had a chance to play in the best league in the world and turned down a second chance. "The goal is very important and I think it is awesome for anyone to experience. But in the end I think the mentality to be able to be up there and see what it takes to be up there [in the NHL] means more than that goal."

CHRISTIAN THOMAS

More often than not, when a player scores his first NHL goal, you'll hear this common refrain from one of the announcers: "It may have been on a rebound, but he can tell his kids it was a breakaway." Most goals in the NHL aren't pretty, and even fewer first NHL goals are beauties. Maybe it was banged in on a rebound or it deflected off a player's leg. This was not the case with Christian Thomas. His one and only NHL goal was an absolute snipe: "I just tried to shoot it as hard as I could. It was probably the coolest moment of my hockey career," says Christian Thomas.

Thomas scored against Viktor Fasth on February 12, 2015, at the Bell Centre in Montreal. The goal came at 16:25 of the first and gave the Habs a 1–0 lead in their eventual 4–3 loss to the Oilers. The Oilers had just broken out of their zone, but before they reached centre ice they turned the puck over. The puck went back into the Oilers zone, where Thomas picked it up on the left side. He looked toward the net on a partial two-on-one and let a wrister rip from his off-wing. Boom! Top corner. "I was almost in shock. It was crazy. I was kind of by myself after I scored, behind the net."

Thomas took it all in. Twenty-one thousand two hundred and eighty-six Montreal Canadiens fans were going bonkers, and they were all focused on him. "I was looking at the crowd and everything at the Bell Centre. It was definitely a surreal moment."

That goal was a long time coming for Thomas. He was drafted in the second round, 40th overall, by the New York Rangers in 2010. He played in his only game with the Rangers a couple of years later before he was shipped to Montreal in a July 2013 trade. He spent most of the following season in the minors but made his way onto Montreal's fourth line for an 18-game stint in 2014–15. "Playing on the fourth line, it was tough to get the best opportunities to score; [to get] a good amount of minutes to get constant chances."

That night, though, in game 12 of his 18-game stint with Montreal, when the Oilers turned the puck over, Thomas jumped on his chance. "It was definitely a lot of relief to score. After that you get a bit of confidence. You didn't get much opportunity to play each game. I had a couple chances before and the puck not going in was frustrating, so after that I felt great."

When Christian Thomas headed back to the American League after those 18 games, he went back with that lone goal. Fast-forward four years later, and Christian Thomas stepped off a plane at midnight. He was two hours east of Moscow in the city of Chelyabinsk, Russia. "Coming off a plane in Chelyabinsk at 12 at night and getting picked up by someone from the team was . . . umm, I don't want to say scary, but I was a bit worried there wasn't much going on."

The former Montreal Canadiens forward who also had NHL stints with the Rangers and Coyotes was now a Chelyabinsk-to-Moscow-to-Warsaw-to-Toronto flight away from home. He was set to play in the KHL. "The hockey was really good. The coach, although he couldn't really speak to many of the players, he trusted us. He let us play our game. It was really fun at the rink. We got treated well. For bad things I'd say some of the meals we had on the road, a couple of places, the hotels were not so good. I mean there weren't too many bad things. It was a good experience."

"I heard a couple of stories that really wouldn't make sense in North American–style hockey or wouldn't happen down here. But all the stories I've heard [about the KHL] I can see being true, but I haven't had many crazy ones."

Hockey is a kid's game, but the NHL is a man's business. When Christian Thomas scored for the Montreal Canadiens, it was a childhood dream come true. He was under the bright lights of the NHL, playing in the best league in the world. That dream didn't last long, though. And when the dream of the NHL ended, the business side of the game brought Thomas to Russia. By the time Thomas was 24, he had settled into a role: if he was going to stay in North America, chances are he would spend his winters shuttling between the NHL and AHL. He chose to go overseas. "The decision to play in Europe, you almost feel like you're not giving yourself a chance to play in the NHL anymore." It was time to a make a business decision.

But when Thomas made his decision to go to Europe, it came with an asterisk. And that asterisk kept the dream of hockey alive a little longer. Christian Thomas was not going to go to Europe right away. Luckily for him, his timing was just right. His NHL window may have been closing, but an Olympic window was opening up. "I signed an American League deal because players with NHL contracts or two-way contracts could not be chosen for the Olympic team. I decided to sign with Wilkes-Barre."

It was so long, Montreal and New York City, and hello, Wilkes-Barre, Pennsylvania — population 40,806. The Penguins gave permission to Thomas to try out for Canada's team for the 2018 Olympics. "We talked to Billy Guerin and we agreed: if I get a chance to play in tournaments during the year or if I get chosen to play for the Olympic team, I could leave the team to go play. He said absolutely. So, it was a great fit there."

Thomas played in a couple of tournaments with Team Canada leading up to the Olympics. Then he waited. He waited for a call to tell him that he'd be on his way to Pyeongchang to wear the red and white for Canada. He got the call midway through the season. The call came with a twist. The news that he was going to the Olympics wasn't only delivered by the Team Canada management: Thomas's father was also on the call to give his son the news. Christian's dad, Steve, scored 420 more career NHL goals than his son. Steve Thomas played in 1,235 NHL regular-season games, and now he got to tell his son he was going to the 2018 Winter Games. "My dad was on the conference call with everyone from Team Canada. He said I made the Olympic team. It was crazy!"

Christian Thomas was off to the Olympics. His dad watched from the stands as he scored one goal and one assist in six games and helped Canada win a bronze medal. "I guess the moment I remember most was the opening ceremony. It was so crazy that I was a part of that experience. Walking around representing Team Canada with the other athletes: the skiers, the snowboarders, the figure skaters."

"The first game putting on the Olympic jersey, I thought, 'This is cool, I never expected this.' It's like a dream come true when you play your first shift in the first period. But then, after that, I felt like it was just hockey. You play the game and you play for Team Canada. They have high expectations and you're excited to play. It was probably the coolest thing I've ever been part of, for sure."

The following season did not have the romance of the Olympics or the romance of the NHL. It was hockey and business. The business side of the game pushed Christian Thomas across an ocean. Thomas landed in Sweden. But not for long: he only played in the Swedish Elite League for two months before he signed with Chelyabinsk of the KHL. Thomas was a long way from his one goal at the Bell Centre and he knew it. But life in the KHL has given Christian Thomas something he didn't have in North America: stability. It did not make his decision any easier. "At 26 years old, I had to make that decision. It's really tough, but it's a really good league where I am in Russia and you kind of get used to the lifestyle. It's definitely very difficult, it's almost hard to explain the kind of decision it was."

It's that lingering thought that you've closed the door on your NHL future that makes the decision to leave North America so tough for so many players like Christian Thomas. Kids who grow up in Canada dream of a life in the NHL, not in Russia. That dream is still alive for Thomas, who put up 19 points in 35 games in his first KHL season. "There are guys who come back and play in the American League or the NHL again, but I guess that doesn't happen too often. For me I think it was a good decision. I like where I am. I like where I'm playing. But if I get another opportunity to come back home and have a chance to play in the NHL again . . . it's definitely still a dream."

Thomas may be a "to be continued" story. He is by no means over the hill. He wouldn't be the first guy to head over to the KHL to return to the NHL (see Giordano, Mark). Right now he has one NHL goal, and perhaps one day he can ruin this book and add one more to thin out that gap between him and the old man. His career has taken him to all sorts of places so far; who can predict if a return to the NHL isn't in the cards one day? "It's been a roller-coaster ride, it's crazy. I've signed for two more years in Chelyabinsk. At least I know I'll be there for a couple more years, but you never know what can happen in the hockey world."

105

Christian
Dube
Right Wing
Height: 5' 11"
Weight: 170 lbs.
Shoots: Right
Born: 4/25/77
Sherbrooke,
Quebec

Highlights:
10/16/96 – With a
little help from the
game's all-time
assists leader
Wayne Gretzky,
Dube scores his
first NHL goal.

Upper Deck and the
card/hologram combination

CHRISTIAN DUBE

When the 1995–96 CHL Player of the Year picks up the phone, he's in a place where you'll find just about any hockey dad: in a rink, watching his son's practice. The only thing that makes Christian Dube a little different from most Canadian hockey dads is that he's an ocean away, in Switzerland. "I said I wanted to go to Switzerland for a year, and 20 years later, I'm still here," he says.

When Dube was his son's age he was dreaming of a life in the NHL. As a kid, he was a Wayne Gretzky fan. A few years later, still in his teens, Dube found himself on the ice at Madison Square Garden. He was on a Rangers power play with his childhood idol: "It was the fourth game of the season. I was the youngest guy on the team. I was 19 years old at the time, playing on the fourth line and a bit of power play," begins Dube, who had 145 points in 62 games the previous season with Sherbrooke of the Quebec junior league. "For me, it was a dream come true, to be honest. I had a poster on my wall of Wayne Gretzky when I was young. He was my idol. Just to play with him was unbelievable."

On this October night early in the '96–'97 season the Rangers were taking it to the Pittsburgh Penguins. The Blueshirts had a 7–1 lead with about 90 seconds to go in regulation, and Dube was planted right in front of Penguins goalie Tom Barrasso: "It was a rebound goal. I was in front. Gretzky made the pass to [Alexander] Karpovtsev at the point. He took a one-timer and I banged at the rebound. I dove. I just dove and I was able to put it in."

"Christian Dube — the 19-year-old on the power play," said play-by-play announcer Gary Thorne.

Dube high-fived his teammates, including Wayne Gretzky. "It's joy. It's like a dream come true. As a kid you dream of playing in the NHL, and my idol was on the ice with me when I scored." He made his way down the Rangers bench, giving out more high-fives. Mark Messier grabbed him and rubbed his head. The fact that Dube had just scored his first NHL goal was not lost on his Rangers teammates: "We had a veteran team, so they knew what it felt like to score your first goal in the NHL."

The moment was not lost on Dube, either. "I played against Mario Lemieux that night. My parents were in the stands for that game. They came to watch maybe three games that year, and they were at that game. That was special for me. That was an unbelievable feeling."

When you look at the players Dube celebrated his first NHL goal with, it is almost stunning that they were all on one team: Gretzky, Messier, Robitaille, Leetch, Graves, Kovalev, Richter. That Rangers team was stacked. They were basically an All-Star team. That sounds like a great team to play on. Sure, it would be a thrill, playing with your idols, but it also made it pretty tough for a kid to break into the league. Add in the fact that this was before the salary cap era, which meant the Rangers could load up on stars whenever they wanted. That's not ideal for a teenager. "The Rangers would try to stack up the team every year to go to the Stanley Cup. It was tough for a young guy to break through and play a regular shift."

Just before Christmas rolled around, Dube was loaned to Canada's World Junior Team. He finished tied for the team lead in scoring with seven points and helped Canada win gold. After the World Juniors he split the rest of the season between the Rangers and the Hull Olympiques, where he won a Memorial Cup. The following year, he spent his first entire pro season in the AHL with the Hartford Wolf Pack. In the second pro season, he was called up now and again to the Rangers, for six NHL games, but he spent most of the year riding the bus in the American League. That was more than enough for Dube: "In the minors I was one of the best on the team in Hartford. It's just that I wasn't having fun playing anymore. I would get called up that year and not play a shift. And then you get called up, you play eight games, and you play two or three shifts a game. That's no fun for a player like me."

"I was 21 or 22 and I was sick and tired of being in the minors. And the thing is I had a Swiss [hockey] licence that changed everything. I had offers with pretty good money, so I said yes [I'll go]. I cannot stay in the American League and just die there."

That Swiss licence came courtesy of a move his father, Norm, made when Christian was just a kid. His dad, a former pro in the NHL and WHA, played in Switzerland in the early 1980s. Christian played hockey in Switzerland while he was growing up. That made Christian Dube a non-import player as far as Swiss hockey was concerned: "It was a huge opportunity. But my dad never thought about it when he came here. It was in the early '80s. Jacques Lemaire brought him here. We didn't even know that when you start as a Swiss [player], it means you get that licence faster. It was a lucky move, I guess."

That lucky move turned into a 16-year career in the Swiss League. And now, here we are a couple of decades later, and Dube is running HC Fribourg in the Swiss A League. His official title is sports director; in other words, he's the boss. His two sons play, and if they are lucky enough to play pro like their father, they too will be non-imports in the Swiss League. Dube owns a home in Switzerland, lives there year round, and visits Quebec in the summer. Dube's one NHL goal was a long time ago and an ocean away, when he was dreaming of life as a full-time NHLer. It's funny where the game can take you: "I was fortunate: I played in two World Juniors, I won a gold medal. I won Canadian Junior Player of the Year, and the competition was stiff — they could have picked Jarome Iginla. I won the Memorial Cup. I was pretty fortunate to win almost everything back in junior. But your first NHL goal is also an unbelievable feeling. It's something that you've been dreaming about for years as a child and then you get there and you score that goal and your parents are there to see it. And I had Gretzky on the ice with me. It was a dream come true, for sure."

PAUL HOUCK

It was one of the most iconic voices in hockey. And if you grew up in Canada in the '60s, '70s, '80s, or '90s, you knew it. You heard it pretty much every Saturday night. But the voice didn't belong to Bob Cole or Danny Gallivan. And the voice, for a lot of hockey fans, didn't even have a name to accompany it. But you heard that voice whenever you tuned into a game from Maple Leaf Gardens. It belonged to public address announcer Paul Morris. He was the PA announcer for close to sixteen hundred straight Leafs home games from 1961 to 1999. His almost monotonal delivery was unmistakable. And on March 26, 1986, Morris said the words "Minnesota goal scored by No. 37, Paul Houck, assisted by No. 28, Mats Hallin, and number sixteen, Marc Habscheid."

"I tried to imitate his voice a few times. I actually have my goal on video and I've sent some guys that PA announcement on voicemail over the years: 'The Minnesota North Stars goal.' That's an iconic voice, for sure. It was a voice that you just knew so well," says Paul Houck.

The goal came in Houck's second NHL game. The former NCAA champ with the Wisconsin Badgers was up with the North Stars on an emergency call-up. After just one more game, a healthy body returned for the North Stars and Houck was sent back to the minors. "Looking back now it's just part of the process. But at the time, I was on a 40-goal pace there after two games," jokes Houck.

The next season was another up-and-down one for Houck. He would get called up and sent back down to the minors on a regular basis. He dressed for 12 games with Minnesota in '86–'87 and watched several more from the press box. The up-and-down life-style of an NHL tweener was a long way from the stability he had with the Wisconsin Badgers during his college career, where he scored 177 points in 165 games. During his first season in Madison, he was coached by the legendary "Badger" Bob Johnson before the coach moved on to the Calgary Flames. "A lot stands out. He was a funny guy. You'd sit and talk to him and you'd be bruised after talking to him because he'd be banging you on your arm all the time. He was one of the most optimistic men I've ever met. He was totally positive. He loved to win and he loved the game."

Johnson loved the game so much that he'd gather his team for a shinny game on Sundays. In college, Houck and his teammates played on Friday and Saturday nights. After the games, some of the boys would go out for a few pops. Well, on Sunday, Johnson would play in what the team called "The Russian Game." Johnson would put on an old CCCP jersey and select the teams. He always made sure the players on his team were the ones who opted out of Saturday's post-game festivi-ties. "He knew the guys that didn't go out, so he picked them for his team. And they would feed him the puck. He scored all the goals. The guys that were out late were on the other team. They'd be lazy and not working as hard, so he'd pick his boys so he'd have success. It was pretty funny."

After his senior season at Wisconsin ended, Houck signed with the Edmonton Oilers, the team that drafted him 71st in the 1981

Draft. His assignment was to head to Halifax and suit up for the Nova Scotia Oilers. Houck was used to playing in front of nine thousand screaming fans and a 40-piece band in Wisconsin. In Halifax, on a good night, two thousand very quiet fans would calmly watch the Oilers in the nine-thousand-seat Halifax Metro Centre. This was pro hockey for Houck: "I went to Halifax in March when the season was sort of dying down. Guys are just kind of thinking, 'Let's get out of here.' It was that kind of thing, you know? It's depressing. I was fired up to start my pro career, and then you get into this sort of thing where it's a notch down in the energy level. But it's the process, I guess."

The size of the crowd, though, didn't really matter. Houck still had a job to do. "You played against guys who were big and strong and smart and quick. It was good. I felt comfortable." But unfortunately for Houck, he says, Oilers head coach Larry Kish wasn't a big fan of his game: "The coach obviously wasn't comfortable with me. I didn't get a whole lot of ice time. It was frustrating in that aspect as well, but the level of play was very good."

Houck scored a grand total of one goal in his 10 regular-season games with the Nova Scotia Oilers. Things looked bleak. How could the former college offensive force make the mighty Edmonton Oilers if he couldn't even get into the lineup in Halifax? Then, on May 31, 1985, a blessing. Paul Houck was sent to Minnesota for veteran goalie Gilles Meloche. "It was great. It was something that I relished. It was totally positive. I wanted out of Edmonton, and not just because I didn't want to go back to where Larry Kish was the coach; it was to get a chance [to play]."

It was a fresh start in Minnesota for Houck, but it wasn't a good one. "I had a great training camp. I was sent down the last day. But in my first game in the minors I ran into a goalpost and tore my knee. So I was out for two or three months."

But hey, you have to make the most out of a bad situation. Minnesota wasn't all that far from where Houck went to school in Wisconsin. Houck was given permission to head to Madison and do his rehab there. It was back to school for Houck, without the classes. "It was great. I don't know if you read the *Sports Illustrated* polls about the number-one party school in college. Wisconsin ranks up there all the time. It's really a great campus with a great energy. Beer and cheese, right? What else is there?"

That rehab stint led Houck to the March 1986 call-up that produced his first goal. But things just never clicked on a full-time basis with for him with the North Stars. "My demise? I think Lorne Henning was a bit of a proponent of mine. I think he liked the way I played, but the North Stars weren't doing that good and they changed coaches."

Henning was out and Glen Sonmor was in — for two games, anyway. Then Herb Brooks took over. If you're a fan of hockeydb.com, chances are you've stumbled across the roster of the 1987–88 Minnesota North Stars. It is a sight to behold. The page lists the stats of each for the 50 men who played at least one game for Minnesota that season. *Fifty!* Paul Houck was one of them. He played in one game for Minnesota that year. He played another 74 in the IHL, where he had 56 points for Kalamazoo. "That's the year they signed a bunch of free agents, out of college, out of junior, out of everything — everyone got a sniff. It was kind of interesting in the minors. You'd go to the dressing room and a guy's skates were gone and he's not around. You'd go, 'What's going on?' Then he'd be back the next day and another guy would be gone. It was a revolving door. By that time, you're sort of numb to it a little bit. You're disappointed because you think you're doing a good job, but you sort of understand the political aspect of it."

Houck spent one more year in the minors before he called it a day after two more seasons in Europe. He's the first to admit his time at Wisconsin means more to him than the pro teams do to him, no disrespect intended. "Yes, absolutely. You're 18 to 22, pretty formative years. We won a national title. We lost my first year and won my second year. It was by far my fondest [memory] and the best hockey experience that I've ever had."

Long after his playing days came to an end, Houck had another pretty amazing hockey experience. It was on June 30, 2013. His son Jackson was selected 94th overall by the Oilers. The Houcks are the only father–son duo to ever be drafted by Edmonton. "It's a pretty good trivia question now, isn't it? Who's the only father–son duo to be drafted by an NHL team? It was exciting. I had a little side wager with him that I would go sooner than he did. So, it worked out okay. He worked really hard. It was an exciting day for Jackson and the family, for sure."

And then there was that exciting day, once upon a time, when Paul Houck's name was called out by Paul Morris at Maple Leaf Gardens. "It was a neutral zone turnover. Habscheid went wide, dropped the puck to me. I shot and went to the net for the rebound. I slapped a backhand in. It was sort of surreal in a sense. As a Canadian kid, you're thinking Maple Leaf Gardens and everything like that. I scored against the Leafs! It was really hard to contain myself with how happy I was."

The only downside from that night was that the goal cost Houck around $200. But not until after the game. "You had to buy all the veterans beer . . . it wasn't all that bad. It was a Tuesday night or a Wednesday night. It wasn't a big night out, so I got lucky."

CHAPTER FIVE

THE GOALIES

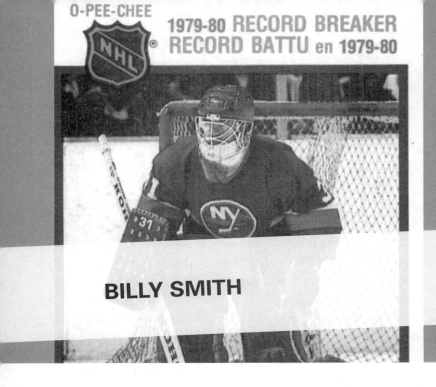

NHL

BILLY SMITH

The first man to walk on the moon? Easy, no? The answer of course is Neil Armstrong. Now name the second. I bet you had to think for a while, if you got the answer right at all. When you're the first man or woman to accomplish a significant feat, your name will live on forever. And that brings us to Billy Smith, the first goaltender to ever score a goal in the National Hockey League. "It's in the record books," says the Hockey Hall of Famer. "So, even with Hexy [Ron Hextall] scoring the second one, it's kind of forgotten. It's always who scored the first. So, in that way, the goal means something."

Billy Smith didn't try to score a goal against the Colorado Rockies on November 28, 1979. His very own perfect storm came 4:50 into the third period. The Islanders were trailing the lowly Colorado Rockies 4–3. Smith didn't even get the start that night. He took over for Chico Resch after he gave up four goals on 21 shots. There was a delayed penalty call on the Islanders' Mike Kaszycki. The Rockies, however, had possession of the puck. Their tender, Bill McKenzie, headed to the bench for an extra attacker. The puck worked its way to Rob Ramage, who let a shot go from the right side. Smith made the save. The puck quickly made its way back to Ramage in the right corner: "He grabbed it and fired the puck back to the point, but there was nobody there. It went all the way down the ice and into the net."

Right away, Billy Smith knew he scored. "I knew I was the last guy to touch the puck, but they gave the goal to one of my teammates." Smith didn't make a big deal out of it because . . . frankly, it didn't seem like much of a big deal at the time. "It's more of a big deal now," says Smith. "I mean, it was pretty neat. Back then it was like, well, we played the game, we lost, so really I wasn't that interested."

After the game, the goal was eventually rewarded to Smith. When you watch the video of the goal it is blatantly obvious that he was the last Islander to touch the puck. So give the NHL credit, they were quick to right their wrong. But it is kind of strange that none of Billy's teammates picked up on the fact that the goal was his. The 7,112 fans in attendance didn't seem to notice either. And like Billy said, he didn't really seem to care either, it's not like he made a beeline to grab the puck. He was the first goalie in the NHL to score a goal — but hey, no big deal. "They kept playing the game with the puck. It ended up going out of the rink. I guess the guy who got the puck ended up sending it to the Hall of Fame."

At least one person in attendance at the McNichols Sports Arena seemed to care that history had just taken place. Over the next few seasons, Billy Smith didn't care about scoring goals. He just cared about winning cups. He won his first of four straight Stanley Cups with the Islanders that spring. As his playing days went on, Smith saw his position evolve. Goalies got better and better at handling the puck. He knew the day was coming. He knew another goaltender would find the back of the net: "You knew just by being in the league and how well the guys could shoot the puck [that it would happen]. In my day nobody wanted the goalie to handle the puck. It was 'Set it up at the side of the net and get out of the way, play your position, and we'll take care of the rest.' But then you got guys like Hexy who could really shoot the puck and it became, 'Okay, if the puck is dumped in, we'll hold the guys back and you grab the puck and fire it out.'"

That's exactly what happened on December 8, 1987, in a Flyers / Bruins game. With the Boston goalie pulled, the Bruins dumped the puck into the Philly zone just to the left of Hextall. The Philly players held the Bruins' forecheck back, Hextall picked up the puck, wristed it about 200 feet and into the empty cage. Voila. Ron Hextall joined Billy Smith as the only goalies in NHL history to score an NHL goal. Unlike when Smith scored, everyone in the arena that night, and everyone in the hockey world that night, knew Ron Hextall scored. The crowd went nuts. The Flyers bench emptied and everyone mobbed Hextall. It was a *big* deal. That just wasn't the case for Billy Smith in 1979: "You know what? Nobody really said anything. We lost when we shouldn't have lost. To be honest, nobody cared. Nobody ever said anything about it. It kind of rolled off our shoulders."

For those of you wondering, Hextall is not in this book, because he scored another goal, on April 11, 1989. That one came in Billy Smith's final NHL season. Again, it was a big deal. "It was funny because when Hexy scored the second one, he got a car and I just looked at our guys. I mean, I didn't get diddly."

Eventually Smith did get something, but it was still pretty much diddly. But at least it came right from the president of the Islanders: "Bill Torrey bought a miniature [toy] car for me."

CHRIS MASON

You would think that being among the small group of goalies to actually score a goal in the NHL would be a big deal. That is, until you talk to Chris Mason. He elaborates: "I just don't feel like I scored one, you know. Honestly, it's kind of cool to have credit for a goal, but it really just doesn't matter to me at all. Sorry — it's not that exciting."

The reason Mason doesn't feel like he scored a goal is . . . well . . . because he didn't exactly snipe one. "Everyone goes, 'Oh, Chris Mason scored a goal!' Everybody always assumes that you fired it down [the ice]. They say 'What happened? What happened?' I tell them, 'You don't even want to know. It's so boring.'"

To be fair, Chris Mason did not whip the puck down the ice and into an empty net like Ron Hextall or Martin Brodeur. His goal was of the Billy Smith variety and it goes like this: On April 15th, 2006, Mason was minding his own business in the third period of a game against the Phoenix Coyotes. A penalty was coming up on the Preds, the ref was waiting for Nashville to take possession so he could make the call. That's when the Coyotes came rushing up the ice. With their net empty in favour of an extra attacker the Coyotes' Geoff Sanderson crossed the blue line and let one rip. Mason made a blocker save and deflected the puck into the corner. Phoenix took possession, the play continued and the Coyotes worked the puck back to Sanderson: "He was trying to go to the point, and the puck bounced over the guy's stick and then it went in."

Yes, the puck sailed all the way down the ice and into the empty Coyotes net. Phoenix coach Wayne Gretzky frantically began waving his arms to the refs, signalling no goal. Perhaps he thought the play should have been blown dead when Mason made the save. It didn't matter, the goal counted; it was just a matter of who would get credit for it. "At that time, I actually thought I might get credit for the goal. But then they announced it, I thought, 'Oh, maybe it didn't happen that way.'"

Vern Fiddler got credit for the goal. "I was like, whatever, he needs it more than I do. It really wasn't a big deal [to me]," says Mason. But on the broadcast, during the replay, Phoenix broadcaster Darren Pang was left wondering if maybe the goalie scored a goal: "You know, it might be Mason's goal," Pang announced. Eventually the play was reviewed, and it turned out that Pang was right: it was Chris Mason's goal. Vern Fiddler was stripped of a goal and Chris Mason was awarded the first goal of his NHL career. All he could do was laugh as the crowd went wild: "I thought it was funny. I just kind of put my arms in the air like, 'Sure, I'll take it,' kind of thing."

Chis Mason did not go wild. He did not have the celly to end all cellies. In fact, just like today, it seems he didn't really care that he scored at all. Perhaps Mason had that attitude because he had a moment like that one before. Five years earlier in an American Hockey League game, Mason scored a goal for the Milwaukee Admirals against the Utah Grizzlies. And just like his NHL goal, his AHL goal was not a classic either. It was the same type of play.

He was the last player to touch the puck before the opposition shot it into their own net. "I got one the same way in the American League, that's what I find funny. I was not a great puck handler by any stretch, so the fact that I got credit for a goal in the American League and the NHL just makes me laugh."

Mason, like every other goalie, wanted that classic goalie-type goal; he just didn't get it, twice. Mason laughs as he tells me on the phone: "If I'm going to score a goal, I want to fire it down and sauce it over the D-man and into the empty net. I always said that maybe I can change the story once I become a grandpa."

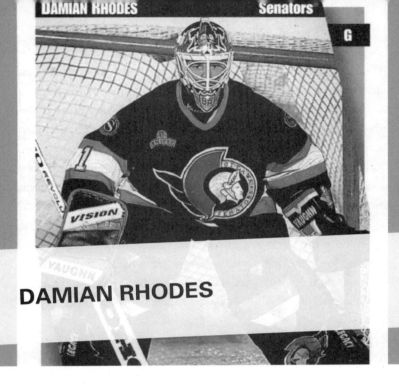

G

DAMIAN RHODES

Ron Hextall could handle a puck. Martin Brodeur could handle a puck. They both scored goals in the NHL: two for Hextall, three for Brodeur. If you were to go down the list of goalies most likely to score in a game, those two tenders would be right at the top. And then there is Damian Rhodes: NHL sniper. Damian admits he would not be at the top of most people's goalies-most-likely-to-score list: "Scoring a goal was never on my mind."

And that's because Damian Rhodes was a righty. That presented a problem. You've seen Curtis Joseph and his patented backhand scoop; well, that's the world Rhodes lived in. He was a right-handed shot in a left-handed goalie world: "I was jealous of the goalies who played left-handed and shot left-handed."

Rhodes wasn't out to perfect the art of the Cujo backhand. In fact, when he played for the Leafs early in his career, his goalie coach, Rick Wamsley, set out to turn Rhodes into a left-handed shot. "We worked on playing the puck a lot and Rick said, 'You gotta play it left-handed. It will be way quicker.' So, I worked on it and worked on it. I got better at shooting left-handed, but those guys who actually shot left-handed could really wing the puck."

Rhodes stayed lefty throughout his NHL career. He says there was no way he could ever lift a puck down the ice. "I would have never got a penalty for shooting the puck over the glass, for sure." So he didn't have a big shot as a lefty. He wasn't going to fire one down the ice for a goal or even an assist. When it came to handling the puck, he kept things simple.

"I made it as simple as possible. I talked to my team about it. Every time the puck was dumped in I told them I would set the puck up for them or I would shoot the puck back the way it came in. I was consistent the whole time. I felt like the sooner I could play the puck once it hit my blade, the less trouble I could get in. So, that's what I did."

So when the night of January 2, 1999, rolled around, Damian Rhodes was thinking what he always did when he stepped on the ice: stop the puck. And, as always, the thought of scoring a goal in the NHL was the furthest thing from his mind. However, with the Senators leading the Devils 1–0 in the first period, the stars aligned. A penalty was coming up on the Sens. The Devils pulled their goalie for an extra attacker. Their net was empty. "I always played well against New Jersey. They had a bunch of shots early. There was a delayed penalty and I blockered the puck to the corner and then I got on my post. Lyle Odelein got the puck and fired it down to his point man and missed him. Then we just watched the puck in slow motion go down to the net."

As the puck slid down the ice, Rhodes only heard one voice. He didn't hear screams from the crowd. He didn't hear screams from his teammates. The only voice he heard was the voice of veteran NHL referee Don Van Massenhoven: "While the puck was going down, he was watching it. He said, 'Rhodesie, that's going to be your goal.' It was like no one else was speaking on the ice when Donnie said that."

And then it happened: the puck slid into the empty net. Rhodes didn't have to wait to find out if he would be awarded the goal. Van Massenhoven had already spilled the beans. The left-handed shooting, right-shot goaltender was an NHL goal scorer: "It went in, and my teammates scrummed around me and patted me on the head. I heard the announcement over the PA. It was a little surreal."

"To be honest, I was mostly unaware of what was going on. I never thought it was a history-making thing. But I guess when stuff like that happens you never think like that."

To make the night even better for Rhodes, he ended up with a shutout in the 6–0 win. You can't help but wonder . . . Rhodes's goal made it 2–0. Did he ever think of letting just one slide by so that his goal would have stood as the game winner? "I never did think of that. As a goalie, a shutout is much more gratifying for you. A goal is such a rarity. I probably had more bonuses in my contract for a shutout than a game-winning goal. It never crossed my mind. That may have been my only shutout that year."

Rhodes didn't chirp any of his teammates after the goal. With his single marker on the season, he was outscoring a couple of other Sens. But maybe Rhodes didn't chirp anyone because this was old hat for him. It was his first NHL goal, but he also scored one in college when he played for Michigan Tech. And he scored the same way: he was the last player on his team to touch the puck before it slid down the ice into an empty net. There was a bit of chirping from his teammates back in college when he scored: "When I scored for Michigan, there was a guy who was a junior on our team named Jeff St. Cyr, and he hadn't had a goal in three years. So, the boys were laying it on him. I didn't even have to say anything because everyone else was saying stuff to him."

Every year around January 2, Damian Rhodes will get a call from a reporter or two who want to talk about the anniversary of the goal. As he says himself, it's his YouTube moment: "It's one of my only YouTube videos out there. Whenever anyone googles my name that goal comes up. People show it to me all the time. Now when I see the video and the PA announcer says that I scored, I put my stick in my holster."

CHAPTER SIX

THE WRONG ERA

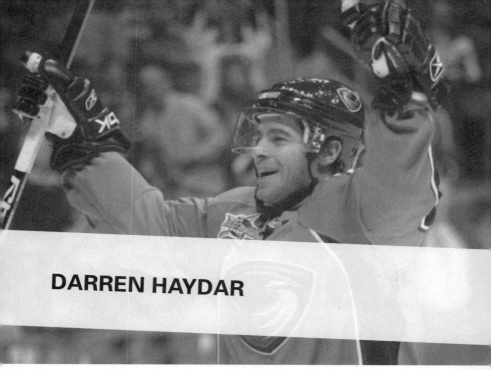

DARREN HAYDAR

When you look at stats on the back of a hockey card or look up a player's numbers on hockeydb.com, you get the raw data. And there's nothing wrong with that. I'm addicted to hockey cards and I'm addicted to hockeydb.com, but there is always a little more to the story than just numbers. Still, Darren Haydar's numbers are astounding: he put up 788 points in the AHL, good enough for fourth all time. He is the AHL's all-time leader in playoff points: 143. He holds the AHL record for the longest points streak at 39 games, and he is a two-time Calder Cup champion. And he scored one NHL goal.

"Brett Sterling got the puck on the left side in our own zone," Haydar begins, almost transforming himself into a play-by-play man. "He chipped it out to Bryan Little. It was a two-on-two. Bryan Little passed it over to me, and then he cut between the D. That caused a little bit of confusion for the defenceman and Brodeur. And I just shot it high blocker side on him. That wouldn't be a spot that I would shoot on a normal occasion. It's kind of ironic how you score a goal in situations where you practise it a hundred times and you wouldn't shoot it in that spot. Fortunately for myself . . . it went in."

And yes, "Brodeur" in this case is Hall of Famer Martin Brodeur. Not a bad guy to score your one and only NHL goal against. That goal came in a 6–5 Atlanta Thrashers loss to the New Jersey Devils on October 13, 2007. Haydar added an assist for a two-point night and was a plus-2. Those numbers may lead you to believe that he felt he was fitting in at the NHL level after years of tearing it up in the minors, but not quite. "For the first 10 games of that year I was almost on a point-a-game pace, and you're still looking over your shoulder as that bubble guy. And I knew that in Chicago [the AHL Wolves], they wanted me back. I felt like it was a matter of time [before I was sent back down] although I was doing fairly well. At no point did I feel like how I would feel on an American League team."

Haydar ruled the AHL. He was a first-unit power-play guy and could play all the minutes he wanted. It just never translated to the NHL. No matter how many points he put up in the AHL, he never made the NHL on a permanent basis. "When I was about 28, 29, I knew I was going to be that bubble guy. I was just looking for that opportunity. I never wished injuries upon anyone. I was waiting for an opportunity."

That opportunity never really came. Haydar put up 202 points in 196 AHL regular-season games in the three seasons following his stint in Atlanta. He only got one more career call up to the NHL — one game for the Colorado Avalanche in February 2010. But still, the numbers don't tell the entire story. Now, if you're wondering why Darren Haydar stuck around the AHL for so long, when a lot of other players like him would head for Europe, a story emerges that you would never find on a stat sheet.

"In 2008 I actually signed a deal in Lugano [Switzerland], but my wife was diagnosed with throat cancer." Haydar made a decision. Europe could wait. He stayed in the AHL while his wife underwent treatment.

"She would have said let's go, but it was more me. I just felt like it was the right thing for our family to be closer to home for treatments. We were going to Rochester, Minnesota, to the Mayo Clinic, for her treatments. I felt like it was the right thing to do. We had health insurance [by staying]. I wanted to make sure she was okay before taking that step [to Europe]."

Darren's wife, Sara, has now been cancer-free for 10 years. As a fan, do you ever really consider what a player is going through off the ice? That's something that is lost on a lot of us, but not on the players themselves, whether they scored one NHL goal or dozens of them. "I think it was Ryan Kesler in Anaheim. People were talking about him getting traded. And he said something like 'Hey, I've got a family. I've got kids.' When this happened, I thought: 'Finally someone is saying this!' As a player sometimes you feel like a piece of meat, and it's not as easy when you have kids to just pick up and go for three months. What do your wife and family do? As a fan, I get it, you want the performance out of your player. But trades are hard on families."

"I hear the fans talking about player X — he's a Ranger, then he gets traded to Buffalo, and all of a sudden he's on fire. Well, maybe he's closer to home. Maybe his family has a better situation. There are so many different variables the fans never see. Again, I get it, they pay the money. They expect a lot. And they should. But former players look out for these issues: why isn't he preforming? What's not right within his family dynamic? There's more than just what's happening on the ice."

Which brings us to 2011. That's when Haydar was diagnosed with multiple sclerosis. "After a game, I think it was the last game before the 2010 Christmas break, I jumped in the cold tub after a game and it felt like I jumped into a bucket of fire. The sensation loss on my left side, it just felt like it was burning."

Haydar got checked out. Then he got the diagnosis. He had MS. Haydar played the final five seasons of his career with MS. And he played with MS while his wife battled cancer as well — things you never see when you look up stats. "Until I finished playing, on my stick I wrote my wife's initials and the date she was diagnosed with cancer, and the date that she finished radiation. You know, you get off a shift and you're yelling at everybody and you're yelling at the ref and I look at the back of my stick . . . and then I think, 'This is just hockey.' A nice reminder of what matters."

During those final few years of Haydar's pro career, he did what he always did — he put up points. He was still pretty much a point-per-game guy, no matter where he played, be it in the AHL, or in Europe, where he finished his career. At around the time when Haydar said goodbye to the game, the game was finally ready to welcome players like him to the NHL. There are a few more numbers on Haydar's hockeydb.com page that stand out aside from his point totals. The numbers are five-foot-nine, 170 pounds. During his career, Darren Haydar was a small man in a big man's game. Now a 170-pounder in the NHL doesn't turn a lot of heads; during Haydar's career, it did. He played in the era of "top six bottom six." That is, your top six forwards better know how to score, and your bottom six better know how to defend or at least rough it up. "What every GM or scout always told me was: 'You need to be in the top six.' I always argued with that idea. I did not just nod my head. I asked them, 'Why can't I be on the third line and be on the second power play, and if you need me, you can use me for the penalty kill? Why can't a skilled player be on the third line? Look at Jiri Hudler. That's how he carved his niche in Detroit.' I tried to get scouts and GMs to see it that way."

Haydar didn't succeed in his arguments. Today he wouldn't even have to put up a fight. He's reminded of just how well he would fit into today's game on an almost daily basis. "I don't want to say it is a daily occurrence, but I definitely hear it a lot." Some numbers on his hockeydb page make you wonder why he didn't get a better shot at the NHL. But again, numbers aren't everything. NHL totals don't mean everything. AHL totals don't mean everything. "Todd Richards told me during my rookie year in Milwaukee that you'll always remember the guys you win with, not so much the guys you lose with. That stuck with me my entire career. The most fun I had were the years we won. My two Calder Cups are up there followed by probably 'the goal.' I would say something else for me that was a highlight of my career was playing on a Spengler Cup team in 2013. That was an experience: I had never worn a Canadian jersey before. The atmosphere, just walking around the town, it felt like a minor hockey tournament on steroids."

The one NHL goal was just part of the journey for Haydar. It was a journey with ups and downs; the kind of ups and downs you can and can't see on a stats sheet. "I got a college education. I definitely wouldn't trade my career for anything. I got to travel the world later on in my career and I helped win a couple of championships. What else would I change, other than an NHL career? But even at that, I definitely enjoyed it. And I'm fortunate. Everyone says, 'Oh, you could have played in the NHL.' To be honest, I was paid to play hockey for 13 or 14 years and I enjoyed every minute of it."

These days, Haydar is a busy man on and off the ice. He sells real estate in the constantly developing Toronto suburb of Milton and trains the next generation of hockey players as a coach. "I'm on the ice more now, I think, than when I played."

And his health? At the moment, it's as good as it can be. "MS is different for everyone. One day you could wake up with your vision gone. Your immune system attacks itself and you could be in a wheelchair at some point. I try to take things from a positive standpoint and one day at a time. I've been fortunate so far to have very limited symptoms. I try to be proactive. I did stem cell therapy in Panama last year."

For Haydar, 2007 and that Thrashers-versus-Devils game was a long time ago. It was a career ago. It was before something that once seemed to be so important, hockey, was put into perspective by life-altering health issues. And "the goal?" It still hangs around — literally. "The puck is in my office. Atlanta did a nice thing. They framed it. They put a picture with it and the game sheet."

MICKI DuPONT

"I think I've played a thousand pro games now, so it's not really something I think about all the time." Those are the words of one-time Calgary Flame Micki DuPont, a few weeks after wrapping up his 19th full season of professional hockey.

"In the memory bank, there's nothing special about it. I mean, you're just playing a hockey game; it's just another hockey game . . . but it was my first and only NHL goal," DuPont says. He says those words without any sense of *Gosh, what a thrill* in his voice. He'll leave that to the sportswriters, I guess. There are, I'm sure, millions of hockey fans out there and thousands of players who dreamed of scoring even a single goal in the NHL. Micki DuPont lived that dream, but as we chat on the phone, he makes it clear to me that he doesn't own a T-shirt that says: "HEY, I SCORED A GOAL IN THE NHL."

DuPont scored for his hometown Calgary Flames on October 14, 2002. The immediate thoughts that went through his mind were not that a dream had just come true: "You're so young

— you don't really think too much about it. You're wrapped up in the game, too. I can't remember exactly [what I was thinking], but I think it was to tie the game at that point, so that was kind of the first thing that went through my mind. 'Hey, we tied the game. Wait a second, that's my first NHL goal.'"

He was taken by the Flames with the 270th pick in the 2000 Draft. If you think there was any pressure on a hometown kid . . . no, DuPont did not look at it that way at all: "Fortunately, looking back, I was a ninth-round draft pick. When I say 'fortunately' that sounds kind of crazy, but obviously there's no pressure on a ninth-rounder, right? When you're a first-rounder, you'd have to talk to them about the pressure they feel, but I'm sure sometimes the pressure probably gets to them. There's a lot of pressure on those guys. When you're a ninth-rounder, and you start to do well, you just kind of surprise people and they start noticing you. It was good timing coming into that organization. They were kind of struggling at the time."

"I was nine when the Flames won the Cup. I was always a Flames fan. I grew up watching Al MacInnis, the big hotshot D-man. I looked up to him and guys like Lanny McDonald and Jim Peplinski."

For parts of two seasons, DuPont managed to suit up for 18 games with his hometown club. He spent his share of time going up and down between the Flames and their AHL team in Saint John, New Brunswick, where he helped the Baby Flames win a Calder Cup in 2001. It wasn't the travel between one side of Canada and the other that was one of the major challenges for DuPont. Fitting in was; playing your own game in the NHL was. In any line of work when you're the new guy at the office, maybe you hold back a little bit, and the NHL is no different: "You're a young guy and you have these veterans on the team that you don't want to piss off. You don't want to do anything stupid or wrong. It's kind of a bad way to think. You should be a little bolder and not care what other people think. But I think most people do [act] like that."

DuPont left the Flames after the 2002–03 season. He didn't play another game in the NHL until December 7, 2006 — one of three games he played with the Pittsburgh Penguins that year. The next season he played in two games for the St. Louis Blues. By this point, DuPont was a 28-year-old five-foot-10 186-pound defenceman, surrounded by much younger prospects in the American League. "Instead of getting called up, they were calling up some younger prospects. That was kind of a signal for me to go over to Europe and experience something else and have a good life over there and make some good money, too."

"So that's kind of why I went over. It was a little tough at the time to give up on the dream [of the NHL], but I was lucky to get up to the NHL for a handful of games and experience it."

If there was one thing Micki DuPont had plenty of, it was skill. If there was one thing he lacked, at least by NHL standards of the early 2000s, it was size. In the dead puck era, size was a commodity that most defenceman could not do without. A player like DuPont could dwell on playing in the wrong era, but he doesn't do that too much. "Now that you ask, I guess, a little bit. I'm happy with the way my career turned out. But, for sure, maybe with the style of the new NHL, you see a lot of small defencemen making it and having really good careers. I'm sure it would have helped if I was born 10 years later."

DuPont was really just a kid when he scored for the Flames. But even though he was just 21, he didn't seem to get swept up in the magic of the moment . . . he moved on. It's just part of a career that has taken him from Saint John to Calgary to Berlin, with dozens of stops in between. The goal is not, by any means, something which defined DuPont as a player; with a little prodding, though, he admits it is something that stands out, at least just a little bit. "The Flames were great: they took the puck afterwards and they made a plaque for me with a photo and the puck inside of it. I have that hanging in my basement. It's always something that . . . is really special."

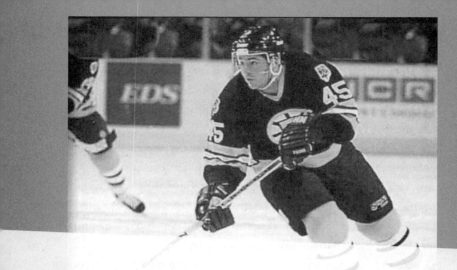

ANDREW McKIM

Christmas for a minor league hockey player isn't exactly like Christmas for you and me. We usually celebrate the holidays at home, surrounded by friends and family. A lot of minor-leaguers celebrate the holidays in a strange town, maybe even in a hotel. If they're lucky, maybe their family is with them. On December 24, 1992, Andrew McKim was in Providence, Rhode Island, set to celebrate the holidays with the woman who would one day become his wife. His phone rang on Christmas Eve. It might as well have been Santa Claus calling, because he was about to get one hell of a Christmas present: "I got called up on Christmas Eve. It was kind of an early Christmas gift."

McKim's holiday plans took an immediate turn. The Bruins were scheduled to play the Hartford Whalers on December 26. Christmas Day featured a ride up to Boston from Providence. "It was kind of a whirlwind because I had to report to Boston. We drove into Boston on Christmas night, got a hotel, and stayed there."

When McKim woke up on the 26th, he had another ride on the I-95. The Bruins cruised right on by Providence as they made their way to Hartford for their game against the Whalers. "To be honest, I don't even remember the bus ride. I sat in [the] front of the bus because I was a rookie. I really don't remember much from that day."

There is something from that day that McKim will never forget. No matter where he played, he put up numbers, massive numbers. He was a top scorer in junior hockey. He racked up points in the AHL, too. In his first NHL game, it was same old, same old, for the Saint John, New Brunswick, product: "I actually scored a nice goal. The puck got dumped into our zone. It went over Ray Bourque's head. I picked it up behind him on our blue line. Actually I went end to end. I went from just the top of our circle, I cut through the middle, I cut to the right side on the outside, cut inside their dot, and I rifled it top shelf over Frank Pietrangelo."

The Bruins won 9–4. McKim was on his way. The kid who racked up 130 points in his final season in the QMJHL was finally in the NHL. But in his fifth game with the Bruins it all went wrong. The NHL was a different place in '92–'93. It was clutch and grab. Elbows were up. Sticks were up. In a January 2 rematch against the Whalers, Hartford's Paul Gillis caught McKim with the wood, in a major way. He cross-checked McKim right in the face. "I broke my jaw in three places. It was banged up pretty good. You're excited one day, and then five days later you're in the hospital in Boston and you're out for the rest of the year with a broken jaw. It was a big bone, too. It was a bad break."

McKim's season was basically over. He played in a couple of late-season games in April, but that was it. The word on McKim was out. Super skilled, but he lacked size. Could he really survive in the NHL of the early '90s? He knew he could. But in the NHL, in 1993, size did matter. It was simply something McKim, listed at five-foot-eight and 175 pounds, could not control. He had scored at every level: major junior, the IHL, the AHL, and the NHL. It just did not seem to help him much. To NHL GMs, he was "too small." McKim spent the next year going up and down between Boston and Providence: "I really don't talk about my hockey career that much. There was a lot of frustration along the way. You just live through it and play, and you move on. You can't really dwell on things that happened."

"I just came back from a trip to Saint John, and my parents have all these articles about me from when I was growing up. I looked at one particular article and I was really angry in it. In it I said, 'I'm doing everything I can, but I can't grow. It's something I can't do.' It wasn't like I was afraid. I used to block shots. I used to kill penalties. We always won, every team I played with, we were always in a championship position. But there was a lot of frustration because there are some things you can't control. Maybe I should have been a soccer player or a golfer. That was the most frustrating part. If you're a doctor or a lawyer, if you're good at your trade, it doesn't matter how big you are."

"I don't think that chip on your shoulder ever goes away. It's hard to lose that. You're doing everything right. Teams are still signing you; they still want you, but you're still trying to get over that hurdle. I remember other guys getting opportunities ahead of me and I just shook my head."

McKim kept scoring in the minors, but it didn't matter, other players kept getting the call. When the expansion draft rolled around in June of 1993, the Florida Panthers and Anaheim Ducks needed to stock their rosters. Surely they would be in need of a proven goal scorer, even if he was undersized by the standards of the day? No. "Every player who was taken was huge. Every player was a huge player. That was the mentality in the league at that time."

McKim left the Bruins organization when he signed with Detroit in the summer of 1994. He lit it up in the AHL again. He led the Adirondack Red Wings with 94 points in 77 games. He managed to get into two games with Detroit. "I remember the meeting with

Scotty Bowman, when I left [after the two games]. He said, 'You're a great insurance policy for our organization.'"

Those are not exactly the words a professional hockey player wants to hear. McKim was a bubble guy. He was too good for the AHL but deemed too small for the NHL. It took its toll: "I was always kind of that bubble guy on the verge of the National Hockey League and on the verge of the minor leagues. It is not fun. That's the mental toughness that people don't understand, and I was that guy. Nowadays I'd be like a Brendan Gallagher, I think, but it wasn't my time."

In the spring of 1995, McKim played for Team Canada at the World Hockey Championships. Canada won bronze. And, of course, he led the team in scoring with six goals and seven assists for 13 points in eight games. That performance at the Worlds opened the way to Europe for McKim, who was tired of living on the bubble back home. He spent the next season playing in Switzerland and on Canada's national team. In '96–'97 he signed with Berlin of the German League. Of course, he was one of his team's top scorers. Whether he was playing in a tight barn like the Boston Garden in the NHL, St. John's Memorial Coliseum in the AHL, or on the vast ice surfaces in Europe, McKim always found a way to score. "I had the same stats everywhere I played. They were pretty close everywhere I played. Europe was a tougher game to play because everyone could skate. It was faster. A lot of NHLers at the end of their careers tried to go to Europe, but they couldn't play because they couldn't keep up to that level. It was a fast game. It was a good game."

McKim played professionally in Europe until a devastating concussion ended his professional career in 2000. In 892 professional regular-season and playoff games, Andrew McKim racked up 981 points. Five of those points came in the NHL: one goal and four assists. McKim is still at a rink all the time. He is the co-owner of Xtreme Hockey in St. John's, Newfoundland. All those skills he showcased around the world are skills he is now trying to teach to the next generation of players. And he also passes on a valuable lesson: "I've learned now, I tell the kids, don't worry about things you can't control. And that's one thing [my size] that I couldn't control."

CHAPTER SEVEN

THE INJURY BUG

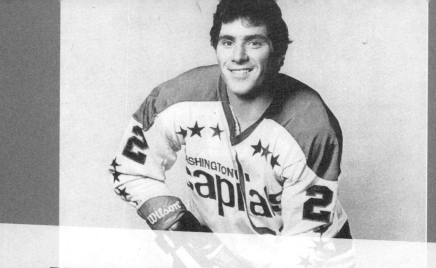

BRENT TREMBLAY

"I didn't know who was on the ice at the time. All I knew was that the puck came back to me at the point off the faceoff. I generally tried to hold the puck out in front of me so I could get it off pretty quickly. But this time I stumbled. I looked up and there was this big green guy coming after me. I knew that if this guy got the puck from me on the point that he would be on a breakaway. I didn't know who it was. I made a move. It looks like it was a Bobby Orr move. But really, I was scared to death. I just stumbled. I had to stop the puck and get around this guy. The move looked like it was planned, but it was not planned at all," begins Brent Tremblay.

The move Brent Tremblay put on that big green guy was world-class. It was, in fact, Bobby Orr-esque. And once Tremblay got around that Hartford Whaler, he let one rip that eluded their goalie, John Garrett, albeit with a little help from the guy who won the faceoff and assisted on the goal, Ryan Walter. "In this day and age, the goal probably wouldn't have counted. Ryan Walter took the feet out from under the goalie."

Brent Tremblay was on the board. It wasn't until later that night, when he saw the goal on TV, that he realized just who he had razzle-dazzled with that move at the blue line. The Whaler that charged at him — i.e., the big green guy that he deked out of his jock — was one of the best of all time. "I found out it was actually Gordie Howe that I had gotten around. It looked like a Bobby Orr move around Mr. Hockey."

"I still have the clippings where Gordie says things like 'The kid got around me this time, but he won't ever do it again.' It's a riot. It was a big deal back then just to have stepped on the ice with guys like Gordie Howe and Dave Keon. It was over the top for me. The moment that I scored the goal, I had no idea that Howe was on the ice. It was just kind of a bonus that it happened that way."

That goal was almost 40 years ago. Brent Tremblay was only 22, but he was already playing on borrowed time. A few years earlier, when he was playing junior hockey with Hull in the Quebec League, he severely injured his back. Tremblay was on a breakaway when he was tripped up and went flying feet first into the boards. "I was on my back, in full flight. I was coiled up. I actually heard my back snap."

After the injury, Tremblay was out of commission for a couple of months. In the following years he played through the pain. By the time he got his second stint in the NHL with the Caps during the 1979–80 season, the pain was almost unbearable: "I was injured when I went up to the Caps, but I couldn't stop. I was fulfilling my dream. You're not going to say you're not going to play. You'd have to pretty much kill me to keep me off the ice. And that was pretty much the mentality back then."

Tremblay would get cortisone shots in his back. The shots only helped with pain for a few days. He kept playing. "It wasn't anybody's fault, really, but my own. I should have taken time off. The doctors would ask me and the surgeons would ask me, 'How do you feel?' I mean, I wasn't great, but I'd look at them and say,

'I'm great.' I just wanted to play. I thought this was my opportunity. I was playing full time."

"My routine was crazy. I'd wake up with pain at five in the morning. I'd jump into the tub. I would put hot water in the tub and just sit there until the pain from the hot water would exceed the pain inside my back. Then I'd go to bed for another couple of hours. I'd wake up and I'd stretch just to make it down to the rink. I'd get to the rink and I'd do 15 minutes with a heat pack, 15 minutes of massage, and then I'd do another 15 minutes of taping. I'd go on the ice and I couldn't walk the rest of the day. It was insane."

It all came to a head one day when Tremblay suffered back spasms before a practice. His body simply told him no. He was put into the hospital. The 22-year-old NHLer had to be wheeled around the hospital by his physical therapist. Surgery was an option, though he never did go under the knife. Still, his NHL days were over.

"It's like a death. It's almost worse than a death because your whole life has stopped. At the time I was looking for a miracle."

Even though Tremblay hoped for recovery, he knew he was finished. "I had no alternative but to re-evaluate everything. I knew that I had to start something new. When you're in that position, you think of anything and everything. I started making pacts with God. I said, 'God, if I can just walk again, I'll be happy. If I can just play on the ice, let me be able to skate on the ice again and have fun with my kids in the future.' Those were the kind of thoughts I had. It was pretty devastating."

When you're 22 years old and all that you know is taken away from you, you can react one of two ways: positively or negatively. No one could really blame a 22-year-old for being bitter; after all, Tremblay's world was taken away from him. "Hockey really was my God. I ate, slept, walked, and talked hockey. Everything. I'd rather skate than walk. That's just where I was. From the time I was three years old, all I wanted to do was play in the National Hockey League. It was all I could think of."

But as they say, everything happens for a reason. "Absolutely. I couldn't really see it at the time, but looking back in hindsight, yes. Put it this way: if you're asking me if I feel bitter, not at all, which is a miracle in itself." In that hospital room, Tremblay found a new God. He had been raised Catholic. He'd pick up the Bible from time to time, but this was something new. His physical therapist would talk to him about God as she wheeled Tremblay down the hospital aisles. Tremblay found something. "My faith gave me peace almost right away. It was kind of strange."

"I wasn't playing hockey anymore. It was still devastating. It was still rough. It was still an adjustment. It's not like I had this aura about me and everything was so peaceful, no . . . it didn't happen like that. It took some time to recover."

Tremblay began training for the ministry. It was his new life. After 12 years, he eventually got back to the game, but hockey wasn't his sole purpose anymore. Missionary work has taken him all over the world. He is now a pastor at the Greenwood Baptist Church in North Bay, Ontario. A few years ago, a friend of Tremblay's found his old goal on video. It's now on YouTube. He fires that video up when he does speaking engagements for Hockey Ministries. That's why his one NHL goal is so fresh in his mind: "It seems like it was yesterday. I've gone to numerous churches all over the place, and I've given my personal testimony about how I became a Christian. It's kind of a good story and I end up doing it a lot. And every time I recount my goal, it's like I'm there again. It's kind of a thrill."

One goal. That was it for Brent Tremblay. One game. Out of his 10 NHL career games, he figures he played a grand total of one game without pain. That one pain-free game was his first NHL game. That was at the Capital Centre in Maryland. The other nine, he was in pain. Massive pain. He did manage to score one goal, before that pain became too much, and his career came to an end. "I'm just so grateful that things worked out. I'm grateful to God for having given me just the opportunity to play. I think had I not had the opportunity even to play at all I would have been disappointed. But the fact that I was playing full time and that I was on the ice and on some road trips with guys and playing — I have these memories and I'm just so grateful, to have stepped on the ice with all these guys. I got to play against the Leafs, for example, and to play against the Canadiens, and to fulfill these boyhood dreams that you had. You can't take it away."

"I'm able to share my faith, just the experience, the wonderful experience of having been able to put the Capitals pants on with stars and stripes, and the sweater, and to be in the dressing room and to have the gates opened up and to get out on the ice and to play this game, to feel the thrill of it all. It's overwhelming. I'm eternally grateful just for the moments that I have. Even though they were short-lived, to have played in the NHL with these wonderful guys and then to have scored a goal against Gordie Howe. What are the chances?"

"It was just a dream come true. I remember sitting on the bench thinking, 'I scored a goal, I actually scored a goal in the NHL.' I'm actually feeling it now."

JOEY HISHON

"My favourite memory of my NHL goal? Jarome Iginla grabbed me. He said, 'Not a bad goal. You'll always be able to remember pulling it around [Shea] Weber, toe-dragging [Roman] Josi and firing it low blocker on [Pekka] Rinne.' To have a guy with that kind of prestige say something like that was pretty cool."

Joey Hishon's first NHL goal was pretty — slick, highlight-reel stuff. He schooled three All-Stars. That's likely the kind of potential the Colorado Avalanche saw in him when they took him with the 17th pick in the 2010 Draft. He was a highly skilled junior and now he was showing it in the NHL. But even at that moment, seconds after his first NHL goal, Hishon knew, unlike a lot of other first time NHL goal scorers, that his first goal would likely not be the first of many. "At that point in time, to be 100 percent honest, I had pretty much come to the conclusion that I wasn't the same hockey player I was before the injury."

The injury was something that altered Joey Hishon's hockey career, but more importantly, his life. "Life in general was so much more important to me at that point in my life than hockey." A few years before he scored his goal, Joey Hishon was in a dark place. "I didn't have the quality of life that I remembered or [that] I was used to. I sat around in a dark room and didn't do anything."

The injury was a devastating concussion that he suffered when he took a vicious elbow from Kootenay's Brayden McNabb in his first game of the 2011 Memorial Cup. Hishon was showing off his blazing speed, cruising up through centre ice. He cut to his left and McNabb caught him with an elbow. "Hishon might be in all kinds of trouble," announced play-by-play man Peter Loubardias. His colour man, Sam Cosentino, immediately added: "He *is* in all kinds of trouble."

Hishon's Memorial Cup was over. Hockey, but more importantly, Hishon's life, was about to change. For the next several months, he basically sat in the dark and did nothing. "There was a long stretch of time where I thought my career was over. I kind of always kept hope in the back of my mind that I'd be able to play again. There were definitely some dark times where I thought I'd never play again."

Hishon did what he could to recover, which at the time, wasn't much. In 2011 the advice from the professionals was to sit in a dark room with no phones and little interaction. Just rest and recover: "And isolate yourself socially. Life was not really fun. You didn't have any connections with people or have the relationships you used to have."

Eventually Hishon started to exercise and in March of 2013, almost two years after that elbow, he played his first professional game when he skated for the AHL's Lake Erie Monsters. He was back, but like he said, the kid who racked up 87 points in 50 regular-season games with the Attack in 2010–11 was now a different player. "Even though I was physically fine and cleared to play, I just didn't feel like I had the same jam that I had before the injury. The mental aspect of it was different. It is hard to explain; just going into a game or different situations on the ice and not having that worry. I was never really the same. Before the injury, if you asked anybody who had watched me, they would say I played with a very high intensity level. After the injury I don't think I had that same intensity level. I just wasn't able to clear my mind and play the way I did before."

But you wouldn't have known that if you watched Hishon's goal against the Preds on April 7, 2015. He scored that goal by doing exactly what he was trying to do before he took the elbow in the 2011 Memorial Cup. He got a head of speed and cut across the ice. This time, he just did what he did so many times before: he flew, he shot, he scored. He finished the play. "Yeah, I was in a territory that I wasn't very comfortable in after that injury."

The goal proved to be the game winner for the Avs that night. Hishon was named the game's first star in his first regular-season game. He had suited up for the Avs in three playoff games the previous season. He did an on-ice interview with the *Star Wars* theme playing in the background. Life was good. When he was asked how it felt to score his first NHL goal, Hishon responded with the usual hockey player answers. But if you watch that interview now, you can see a kid trying to do everything humanly possible not to crack a huge smile. "Absolutely. I think I was pretty much blacked out until that interview and then I started talking again. It was a pretty cool feeling, and even when I think about it now, I smile again."

The clichés Hishon spoke on the ice that night were exactly what you'd expect from a young player. But it is not hard to tell exactly what, or perhaps more importantly whom, he was thinking about. He was thinking about his parents, for one, who had to come up with the cash to keep him playing minor hockey for all those years. And he was thinking about someone else, too. Joey Hishon will tell you there is no way he would have ever scored in the NHL without his wife, Dora. She is the person who finally got Hishon to make his hockey comeback and to move on from that elbow. "She was with me through the darkest of the dark times.

For her to stay with me . . . without her, I'm not sure where I'd be right now. Just to look back at that and realize how important it was for me to have her by my side, and for her to make the decision to stick with me, is absolutely incredible."

"I was spiralling. Without her to balance things out and keep me on the right track, who knows where I could have ended up?"

Hishon ended up where he was supposed to end up, in an NHL arena, celebrating an NHL goal. But as he said, he knew he was a different player. He spent the entire next season in the AHL, where he put up a solid 43 points in 62 games. He never got another call-up to the Avs. Rather than sit around and do the same thing the following season, Hishon headed to Jokerit of the KHL. "Financially, it was a decision I needed to make — to get myself ahead a little bit and start making a little bit of money."

Hishon spent two years enjoying hockey and the lifestyle of a professional hockey player in Europe and then it was over. He retired from professional hockey when he was just 26. "When I was younger, the picture of my world was a little different."

Here's the thing about Joey Hishon. He is so much more than a kid who got hit with that vicious elbow at the 2011 Memorial Cup. He was in the dark. He could have called it quits. His hockey career could have come to an end that day. It didn't. The hit does not define him. His one NHL goal does not define him. But does his comeback define him? It should. That's the part of the story that should resonate with everyone: "I think anytime anybody goes through any adversity and comes out the other side, and has a little bit of success, it feels even better than it would if you went straight there."

Hishon went through unbelievable adversity, and got his goal. He is currently the assistant coach and the assistant GM of his old junior team, the Owen Sound Attack. Aside from some issues with his neck, he feels no lingering effects of the concussion, "Being in the one goal club, I guess it's better than being in the no-goal club."

"I'm extremely happy with what I'm doing now and I'm extremely excited for the future, and hopefully I'll work my way back to the NHL."

DAMIAN SURMA

Have you ever done your best to avoid imminent bad news? You know the story: your boss from work is calling, and maybe he wants you to work a little overtime on the weekend. Of course you end up trying to ignore the call and your boss at all costs. That's what Damian Surma was up to one March day in 2003: "It was kind of hectic, actually. I was supposed to get sent down [to the East Coast Hockey League]. I sort of raised a stink about it the week before. Coach was trying to get a hold of me for about four hours and I wouldn't answer the phone."

Surma's phone was ringing, but there was no way he was going to answer. He was convinced that his assistant coach, Tom Rowe, was set to tell him he was going to be sent from the American League's Lowell Lock Monsters down to the East Coast League's Florida Everblades. That's what his coaches had told him: "They said the plan was to send me down to the East Coast League. I said, 'Well, I've been here all year. I haven't said a word. I'm finally starting to get some playing time and I'm going to go down to the

Coast? No, that's not right.' I told them, 'I'm not going to go.' A week later, my phone was ringing off the hook."

Eventually his coach gave up calling and tracked Surma down at his apartment. "I poked my head out the door and I said, 'Sorry, your number came up as an unknown, so I didn't answer it.'" Rowe stared back and delivered the news in his Boston accent: "You big knucklehead [and Surma is laughing as he is telling me this], pack your bags!"

The reality of what Surma thought was a demotion hit him. "I said, 'How long am I going to Florida for?' He said, 'You're not going to Florida. You're going to Carolina.'" Surma could only say one thing: "'What?' Rowe said, 'Yeah, you're going to Carolina, somebody got hurt.' I said, 'Holy . . .'"

The Carolina Hurricanes were a banged-up bunch in 2002–03. The injury bug bit hard so hard, in fact, that the Canes were running out of roster players. Hence the search for Surma. "I was an emergency call-up. They had another player go down for them. It was a bad year for injuries for the Hurricanes. I think they lost something like 250 man-games to injury. Something crazy like that."

So much for a trip to the East Coast League — Surma went from the nightmarish thoughts of a demotion and getting bagged in the AHL to the big time. "I was still getting skated every day after practice. I thought there was no way this call was about me going up to the NHL. If it was, I would have answered it on the first ring."

Surma suited up for the first game of his NHL career on March 18, 2003, in front of 16,531 Caniacs. He started the night, not surprisingly for a call-up, on the fourth line. But then the theme of the '02–'03 Canes took over. The injury bug bit again. "Josef Vasicek got hurt and went into the room and the coaches said, 'Surms, you're going up next with Ron Francis and Jeff O'Neill.' Instant nervous sweat."

Just like that Damian Surma, the 22-year-old kid who was living in fear of being sent to the ECHL, was on a number-one line in the NHL. And it wasn't just any number-one line. He was being centred by a guy who sits fifth all time on the NHL points list. "I was thinking, 'Oh my God. I'm going be on the line with one Hall of Famer, for sure, and another guy who arguably could have been a Hall of Famer. And one shift in the NHL on the first line and I ended up scoring a goal.'"

Soon after taking to the ice on his first shift with Francis and O'Neill, Surma found himself on a two-on-one. O'Neill was racing with the puck down the right wing. Surma was wide open: "I remember skating as fast as I could up the ice. The whole time I was thinking, 'I can't believe it, I'm going to get a breakaway. He's going to slide it over, I'm going to get a breakaway. I'm going to get a breakaway.' And then he shot it."

O'Neill let one rip. It was a bomb from the right side. Patrick Lalime made the save, but the rebound jumped high in the air. Surma was still in full flight: "The puck was in the air, not in slow motion, but in super slow motion."

That's when Damian Surma's instincts took over. They were instincts from somewhere in his childhood. He did something you don't spend a lot of time working on as a hockey player. Surma reached deep into his mind and did his best Babe Ruth. "I swung as hard as I could." He batted the puck out of the air and into the net.

"It was luck, going full speed and being able to bat the puck out of the air. I played baseball in high school; I was pretty decent at it. I was pretty good at batting pucks down, but going full speed to the net and being able to bat the puck down, and making it look like I was able to put the puck upstairs was just a lucky, lucky coincidence. I was just happy to hit it."

The guy who thought he was going to the deep recesses of the minors was an NHL goal scorer: "I had instant thoughts of everything I ever worked for as a kid growing up and going to play juniors. Everything just came to a head when that puck went in."

Surma's joy didn't last for long. He didn't know it in the immediate seconds after that puck crossed the line. He was hugging his teammates; he was giving out high-fives; but he was in trouble. About 30 seconds after he scored, he knew it: "After I scored I tried to jump over Lalime and he caught my leg. I went into the boards and I blew my shoulder out. It didn't even matter, though. I still celebrated. I had my hands up in the air. I couldn't feel it until I got back to the bench. That just tells you how exciting of a moment it was because I had a shoulder separation and my hands were above my head and I was hugging everybody and giving them fist bumps. I had no idea my shoulder was separated until I got back to the bench."

Surma was the latest in a long list of Canes to go down with an injury. The trainers told him to head to the room for X-rays. He knew he was hurt, but he continued to play. "I should have probably gone back for X-rays. I think it was on my next shift that I tried to hit Zdeno Chara. I caught him with his head down and I've never been hit harder in my entire life. He is the biggest man I've ever come into contact with."

After the game, Surma got his X-rays. He knew what was coming: he indeed had a separated shoulder. "I was on the shelf for a while, and it should have been the rest of the year, but it turned out being 12 days. That old saying — hockey tough — I wanted to come back and show them I could play through pain, play through an injury."

Surma was an emergency call-up for the Canes that night against the Senators, so they sent him right back to Lowell. He suited up for the Lock Monsters less than two weeks after blowing out his shoulder. "My first game back was against Worcester. I ran into a guy and I felt my shoulder give way a little bit. I was pretty much useless the rest of the year."

The fear of demotion, the joy of a call-up, the thrill of scoring in the NHL, a separated shoulder, a demotion back to the farm — all in a matter of hours. It's not like Damian Surma gave up on hockey after that season. He got another call-up the next year. It was for the Canes' final game of the season. "When I got called up then, I *was* in the East Coast League. After our last game of the year, the coach said I was going to play the last game of Carolina's year in Florida because I was in Fort Myers. The Hurricanes were just trying to save money on a flight, so they just had me drive over instead of sending somebody from Lowell."

But Surma made the most of it; he even got an assist. If you look up the numbers, Damian Surma is a point-per-game player: "I may have used that line a few times at the bar, that I'm a point-a-game guy in the NHL — me, Gretzky, and Lemieux," Surma laughs.

In the ultimate game of what-ifs, I have to ask him: "Damian, what would have happened if Jeff O'Neill slid that puck across to you, instead of letting it rip? Would you have scored on the breakaway? Would you have ended up with a separated shoulder when you charged to the net?"

"I would like to think I would have scored on a breakaway. But as nervous as I was, I probably would have missed the net. That puck going up in the air made it the greatest thing that ever happened to me, because I could say I scored a goal in the NHL."

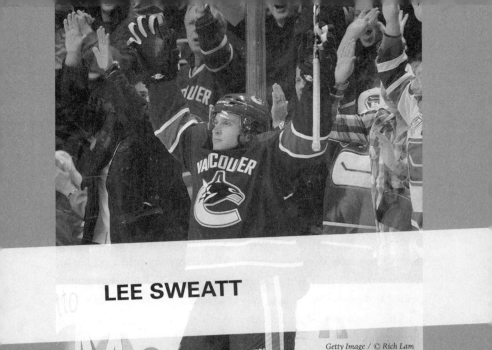

LEE SWEATT

Getty Image / © Rich Lam

Being a healthy scratch on a winter's night in Latvia is a long way from the NHL. But that's where Lee Sweatt found himself during his time with Dinamo Riga of the KHL during the 2009–10 season. As Sweatt tells me, "I was thinking: 'Where is my career going?'"

For the moment, it was going nowhere fast. It seems that every North American who plays in the KHL leaves with at least one story. And here is Sweatt's: "I was performing very well in that league, but the North American imports did not get along with the Russian coach. There were significant communication problems. The team was not playing well. The coach's job was on the line. He could not get rid of the homegrown Latvians, so he put the blame on the imports. The imports . . . we got pushed out a little bit. Sometimes we were healthy scratches, which was odd, because we were the best players on the team. The coach told the press it was all our fault and the imports were the reason we were losing. But the team kept continuing to lose when we were healthy-scratched."

Sweatt may have not got a chance to play in Riga, but he was selected to play for Team USA at the Deutschland Cup. There was just one problem for Sweatt: when he got to Munich, Germany, for the tournament, he was totally out of game shape. "I said to myself — this is bad. I've got to change my situation. Otherwise my career is going to be done."

There was only one option: Sweatt had to get the hell out of the KHL. Like he did a season before when he found himself playing in Austria, Sweatt took action: he bought himself out of his KHL contract. A graduate of Colorado College, armed with a degree in mathematical economics, he added things up and decided to return to the Finnish Elite League. He'd had success in that league before and figured he could do it again. He signed a deal with TPS Turku. "I had incredible success the rest of that year. I was on the power play. I played with Valtteri Filppula's brother, Ilari. He was one of the best playmakers in Europe at the time. It just clicked."

Turku won the league championship and Sweatt was named the Finnish Elite League's top defenceman. That success in Finland was enough to lead him to something he never had before — a North American contract. Sweatt was offered deals from Philadelphia and LA after his third year of college hockey but decided to return for his senior season year at Colorado College. "We didn't have a very good year. We were barely above .500. The team didn't do great, so we didn't get a lot of attention. I kind of went off the radar of a lot of NHL teams." Sweatt landed a PTO with San Antonio of the AHL when his senior season came to an end, but no serious NHL offers were on the table. However, there were still options.

"I'd been going to Europe every single summer since I was 13 to play in the World Championships of inline hockey for Team USA, and I loved going to Europe. So I knew my way around, and I thought, I will play for a European team, live for free, and get paid to play hockey . . . sure, obviously I wanted to get to the NHL, but it wasn't really at the forefront until I stated having some initial success over there."

In the summer of 2010, after four seasons in Europe, the NHL came calling. He signed with the Vancouver Canucks. He spent most of the season in the AHL with the Manitoba Moose. (His brother Bill, a future NHLer, was a teammate.) But Lee did not spend the entire season in Manitoba: in late January of 2011, he got the call-up to the Canucks. The five-foot-nine 195-pound defenceman, who was a healthy scratch in Latvia a little over a year earlier, was about to suit up in the best league in the world.

"My God. Russia was one of the most trying experiences of my life," says Sweatt. "But trying experiences build character and it made the taste even sweeter once that happened. Even just getting on the ice. I'm an undersized guy in terms of height; my whole life, I was told I was too small. I was told I was too small and that I was never going to make it anywhere. I didn't even play triple A hockey until I was at midget major. I played one year of junior in the USHL, and when I signed at Colorado College I was supposed to be a seventh or eighth defenceman."

But now Lee Sweatt was in the NHL. On January 26, 2011, he experienced the ultimate high, followed quickly by the ultimate in pain. In his first NHL game, he scored his first NHL goal: a third-period game winner for the Canucks in a 2–1 win over Nashville. "The pass was incredible. I still watch it every once in a while."

Sweatt's goal was set up by a beautiful, no-look feed from Daniel Sedin. Sweatt took the pass and beat Pekka Rinne with a wrist shot. "It just worked out. I was playing with some of the best players at the time: the Sedin twins; Luongo; and Ehrhoff was my D partner. You couldn't ask for better players to play with. It was really spectacular. Obviously the first game is a huge adrenalin rush the whole time, but scoring that goal was really magical. It really was."

Then came the pain. Sweatt stayed on the ice for the next shift. The defenceman found himself in his own zone. Five days before he clocked a slapshot at 104.9 miles per hour at the NHL All-Star Skills Competition, Shea Weber stepped into one against the

Canucks. Lee Sweatt got in the way: "Weber takes a one-timer and it goes right off the inside of my foot. It was my fault for opening up my foot and not having the plastic guards on it. It was pretty brutal. When you have your foot in your skate after you get hit, the swelling is pretty restricted, you can still work yourself through it for the most part, but then afterwards it was pretty brutal."

The pain was bad, but Sweatt figured he could handle it. The good news for Sweatt and the Canucks was that, thanks to the All-Star break, they had five days between games. When the schedule resumed after the break Sweatt suited up for another two games and played through the pain. Then the bad news: at a morning skate Sweatt took another shot off his foot. That shot did the trick: "Keith Ballard just took a little nothing wrist shot from the point. I was just in front boxing out. Nothing crazy, just a little nothing wrist shot . . . but it hit me in the same spot as the Weber shot, and I buckled. It ended up breaking my foot. The way I see it is that my foot was probably broken from Weber's shot. It's just that the little nothing wrist shot hit it in the right spot and broke it fully."

A broken foot is bad news. But there was some good news for Sweatt. Sweatt didn't know it when he was out on the ice at that practice, but the Canucks had plans for the undersized defenceman. Right after the skate the Canucks had planned to send Sweatt back to the minors, but because he was now injured with a broken foot, the Canucks could not make that move. Sweatt got to stay in Vancouver and collect his NHL paycheque, as opposed to a minor league cheque, for the rest of the season. His year was done due to the broken foot, but at least he was making big-league money for the rest of the year. That summer the Canucks elected not to sign Sweatt. He became a free agent. He signed with the Ottawa Senators on July 11, 2011, but he never made it to the Sens camp. A month after he signed with Ottawa, 26-year-old Lee Sweatt announced his retirement: "What wasn't really reported at the time but weighed heavily on the decision, was that as a pro I had four concussions. In collegiate hockey

I had probably four or five more. I had four that were actual concussions and probably another one in there that should have been registered as a concussion . . . and who knows how many as a kid."

"The decision really came down to the preservation of my brain. At the time, I got a two-year deal with Ottawa, pretty good money, but I was going to be up and down between Bingo [Binghamton], and Bingo just didn't have a whole lot of appeal."

"My longevity outside of the game was [going to be] a lot longer than my longevity inside of the game. So I had to make the decision [that] you know what, I'm not going to sacrifice my head. If someone trucks me into the boards — which in the American League happens literally on a game-by-game basis — I could have been seriously hurt, permanently. In the AHL you get third- and fourth-line guys trying to make a point, [called up] from the East Coast League, running around with their heads cut off. I just made the executive decision; it's not as good money to start my career, but I have to do it at some point. And the longevity of my career, doing what I do now, really drove my decision, coupled with the concussions. Long term, it was the better move."

Sweatt walked away from hockey and became a financial advisor. Throughout his pro career, he wasn't only trying to make himself smarter on the ice; he was trying to make himself smarter outside of the rink as well. From his time in Riga all the way to Vancouver, Sweatt was always reading: "I always valued my education, and I literally felt like I was getting dumber after my first year [pro]. So, to fill my time I checked out the University of Colorado executive MBA program. I applied and I got in. I started doing my first MBA, had even more time on my hands when I was in Riga and travelling through Russia, so I picked up another one. I was actually finishing my MBA while I was playing for the Canucks. It is kind of weird, when you're studying for your finals and you're in the middle of a playoff push . . . but having said that, I ended up getting three MBAs."

Sweatt continued, "You never want to stop playing the game, but you either leave the game on your own terms or the game leaves you. And I didn't want to sacrifice my current career just to get a little extra taste of playing in the show, although I absolutely loved it and it's something I'll never forget. Just getting there was a lifelong goal, and staying there was never really in the cards."

Sweatt had proven his point. He was never drafted — he made it to the NHL. He was too small — he made it to the NHL. He was a healthy scratch in the Kontinental League — he made it to the NHL. He scored in the NHL. "The goal is the culmination of a lifelong goal. It is the culmination of proving everybody wrong: all those people who told me I was never going to make it. I was too small, I wasn't talented enough. I proved everybody wrong. It was literally a release of . . . I won't say anger, but desire and drive for a 20-year hockey career, starting when you were four years old, when you take your first steps on the ice. It's really the culmination of that moment. It's really special. That's where it stands."

CHAPTER EIGHT

FIRST-ROUND EXPECTATIONS

SCOTT METCALFE

Courtesy of the Rochester Americans

A number of Edmonton Oilers greats like to tell a story about Oilers training camp during the Sather years. At a lot of teams' training camps the coach would walk into the dressing room and warn players that any spot on the team was up for grabs. In the mid-1980s, during the middle of the Oilers dynasty, Glen Sather would not play those games. The Oilers' big boss was an honest man. He'd basically tell the troops, look, maybe one spot is available. That's the environment Scott Metcalfe walked into in 1985.

Just a couple of months earlier, the Oilers took the rugged centre with 20th overall pick of the NHL Entry Draft. Needless to say, Metcalfe didn't make the Oilers the fall after he was drafted. But attending camp did have its benefits: "I would go back to junior and on a standard-issue breakout pass, because I was playing at Oilers speed, I'd be on a breakaway by the centre red line. The first couple of games back from Oilers camp, I'd have seven or eight points a game because I was playing at Oilers speed."

Year after year, Metcalfe kept trying to crack the Oilers lineup, but it just didn't happen. He spent his first year as a pro in 1987–88 in the American League. During his second year as a pro, he managed to get into two games in Edmonton. He was surrounded by superstars. "Mark Messier would make you feel like a million dollars when you walked into the dressing room. You'd be just walking off a flight, getting called up. And then he'd make you feel like a million dollars. He'd tell you: 'Don't take a back seat to anybody out there.'"

Those two games in January 1988 were Metcalfe's only with an Oilers team that was on its way to another Cup. There was no room for the first-rounder from 1985. Metcalfe was traded to Buffalo on February 11, 1988. "Buffalo was doing well but struggling to find their identity. It was a totally different feeling in the dressing room. Edmonton was all team and Buffalo was . . . trying to find their way. I think that is the best way to say it."

It was a new organization for Metcalfe, but it was the same old story. He only got into one game with Buffalo after the trade. He spent the rest of the year in Rochester, a place that would eventually become his hockey home. The following year, Metcalfe was up and down between Buffalo and the farm, and he played in nine games in the big league. The best was a New Year's Eve tilt against the Philadelphia Flyers: that's when it happened. Metcalfe was playing his typical hard-hitting and scrap-if-you-have-to kind of game . . . and then he scored: "I went hard to the net. Now, the great thing about the NHL was that when you got open, the puck was on your tape. In the minors if you get open, your teammate may not see you. But in the NHL, 9 out of 10 times that guy sees you. He saw me. I just went to the back door with my stick on the ice. Ron Hextall couldn't get across and I slid the puck into the open net."

"To be honest with you, I was very thankful that my parents were there. But more than anything, I was thinking they can't take that away from me. I got one. Especially with the style I played, the grinding, the goals didn't just come about."

Bryan and June were there to see their son score in the NHL, but there was more: Metcalfe dropped the gloves with Derrick Smith in the second period. The NHL goal scorer caught up with his parents after the game. They dreamed of things to come. "My dad said, 'Son, that was a very good game. They'll have a tough time sending you down.'"

Metcalfe played in five more games before he was sent back to Rochester, a little over a week after his 22nd birthday. He was called up for two more games with the Sabres in late March. Metcalfe had his goal, and as the years went by, he was starting to be looked upon as more of a minor league leader than a prospect. "You have to take pride in it. You have to take pride in being a pro. You can show the kids that there's a lot of pride and a lot of work that goes into being a pro for a long time, show them it's not easy, that you gotta scratch and claw for everything you get."

Metcalfe headed for Europe for a couple of seasons before he wound up back in Rochester in 1993. For the most part, he stayed there for the next five seasons. Retirement came in the early 2000s. "When I was done playing, I pulled my stuff up to my house. We had a nice little house here, just a small one. I looked at my wife and I said, 'Well, are we moving home?' She said, 'We are home.' And that was the end of our conversation."

Scott Metcalfe has been in Rochester ever since. "I'm in the Amerks Hall of Fame, all-time penalty-minute leader and top 10 in scoring. Not too many of those around, are there? I didn't think I had a good season unless I had 20 goals and over 200 PIMs." And don't forget — he had one NHL goal, too.

"I don't think the one goal is good or bad," says Metcalfe. "It's one thing people can't take away. I did get my goal, but at the same time, in a perfect world, you always hope for more. You always dream for more. I had a couple of coffees in the NHL . . . but to be honest, they were great cups of coffee. It was a lot of fun."

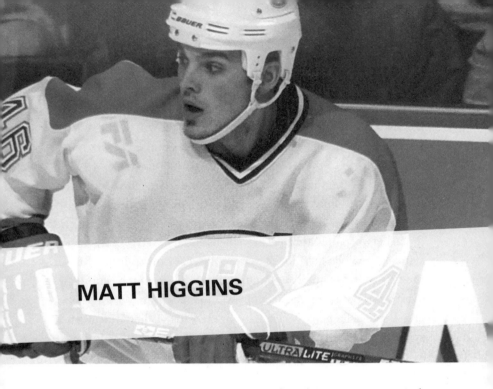

MATT HIGGINS

When you think of life in the NHL, a few things come to mind, like chartered jets, world-class meals, and first-class hotels. You just don't consider the fact that the stays in those hotels could last more than a few days, or even a few weeks. During one of Matt Higgins's stays with Montreal Canadiens, he ended up living in a hotel for five months. "You get to know the cleaning staff," Higgins chuckles when talking about his five months in a single room. "Aw, man, the positive part, I guess, is that I was really close to the rink. I could walk to it every day. You had to make sure you had a little mini-fridge to put everything in and figure out what nearby restaurants could give you a deal. Sometimes it wasn't fun. My advice: make friends and try and maybe have a home-cooked meal once in a while."

Higgins's stay in that Montreal hotel started simply enough. He checked in ahead of camp when he was training in Montreal; stayed for training camp; initially made the Canadiens; and stayed, and stayed, and stayed. He was waiting for the Montreal brass to tell him to get an apartment. But for whatever reason, the news took almost half a calendar year to come. "I actually ended up getting an apartment. I [stayed in the hotel so long] because I was up at the start of the season, I got sent back down, then I was up. I just kept the hotel because all my stuff was in there. I was going back and forth to the AHL. I went up and down a bunch. I stayed in the hotel until finally I was there for the maximum amount of time that was allowed and they had to tell me to get a place."

Matt Higgins spent the early part of his career shuttling up and down between the Montreal Canadiens and the AHL. That is pretty standard practice for a lot of young players. Montreal took him in the first round of the 1996 Draft, 18th overall, from the Moose Jaw Warriors. "I grew up in BC and I was in French immersion school and I spoke French. When they drafted me, I did some French speaking to the media."

Now that is how you win the hearts of the Montreal media. More importantly, though, Higgins had to win the hearts of the Canadiens management and coaching staff. "At that point in my life, there was no real internet, no social media; I'd see the Canadiens once a week on TV. I knew it [going in the first round to Montreal] was a big deal, but I didn't really understand how big it was until I was there."

Higgins turned enough heads to slip into one NHL game during his first year as a pro in 1997–98. The next season, he made the team out of training camp. During his fifth game of his campaign, on October 28, 1998, Higgins's Habs were getting schooled on home ice by the Boston Bruins. It was the first game of a back-to-back against Boston, and the Bruins meant business. They were up 3–0 after the first and 6–0 after two periods. With just under four minutes left to play and the Canadiens down 9–1, Higgins did his thing. "I can actually say it was a nice goal. I came out of the corner, maybe beat a guy out of the corner, came across onto my backhand. Byron Dafoe was the goalie. He made a poke-check move. I went around him on the backhand and scored."

Unlike a lot of guys, when talking about his first NHL goal, Higgins can simply sit back and tell the truth. No exaggeration is necessary: "It wasn't like I scored by the puck going off my shin pad or anything like that, I can at least say the lone goal I got was a half-decent goal."

"I can't really tell you it was magical. We lost 9–2 and we had to get on the plane to head to Boston. It wasn't really as nice as maybe it could have been as far as that part of it goes. I just kind of thought it was my first goal of the year and I'll keep it going, but I never did."

He never did for a variety of reasons. But Higgins can point to one specifically. In November he suffered a concussion. It kept him out of the lineup for a little over two weeks. It was just one of many injuries he suffered as a pro: "I had four back surgeries, two hip surgeries, four other surgeries on other parts. The biggest thing for me was, I got a chance. I got 50-some games, but my body was just never really meant for [the NHL]."

Higgins stuck with the Habs until early January. An injury — or rather, the recovery from an injury — got him a ticket to the minors. Scott Thornton was returning from injury, so the Canadiens sent Higgins to Fredericton in the AHL. His tenure in Freddy Beach did not last long. After just 11 games with the Baby Habs, Higgins's season came to an end. He had to undergo back surgery. "I always think [of a career] as a package. You gotta have the skill. You gotta have the heart. You've gotta have the head and you've gotta have the body. You gotta have the body that can last. That's part of being a really good player, being able to play every game. I just didn't have that part of what you need to play [in the NHL]. To me, to be the package, you've got to be able [to stay healthy]."

Higgins split the next season between Montreal and the AHL. In 1999–00, he was relatively healthy and played in 72 games, the most of any of his pro campaigns in North America. Just six of them were with the Canadiens, though. The remaining 66 were with the Quebec Citadelles in the AHL. After two more injury-riddled seasons in the AHL, where he dressed for 43 and 45 regular-season games, Higgins's body just couldn't take any more of the North American game. He turned to Europe. His NHL career was over: "Europe was a lot easier. We played two games a week and had a 50-game schedule. There was not as much contact and I somehow made it through over there for eight years. I still had some injuries over there, but it was a lot easier on the body."

Of course, Higgins never envisioned his NHL career consisting of one goal — he was a first-round pick, after all. "I guess there are two ways that I can look at having one goal. It's an accomplishment to get the one goal. But obviously, when I started my career I was hoping to get more than just one goal. I look at it now that I'm over 40 and have my kids, I look back and say it is an accomplishment to make it and it is an accomplishment to get the one goal. I'm very proud of that, but obviously deep down I wish I had more than one."

And there's another thing Higgins didn't give a lot of thought to when he was selected by the Canadiens — his health. What 18-year-old *does* think about it? When you're a kid, whether you're a hockey player or not, health is usually, and hopefully, the last thing on your mind. Higgins's body paid the price, though. And now, all these years later, maybe that's what more important to him than scoring an NHL goal: "I think leaving the game healthy after 10 surgeries is another one of the things that ranks up there for me; now that I'm older, it's more important. I had some tough runs there when I was playing. My last year I was healthy, and that ranks up there, too."

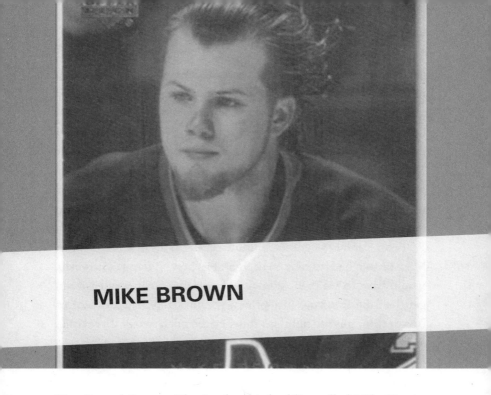

MIKE BROWN

First Round Brown. That's what his buddies called Mike Brown back in junior.

Guys like Mike Brown pretty much don't exist anymore. In his draft year with the Red Deer Rebels, the six-foot-four 220-pound winger scored 19 goals and added 13 assists, in 70 regular-season games. He also fought over 30 times in the regular season and in the WHL playoffs. That spring, Mike Brown got his nickname when the Florida Panthers took him with the 20th pick in the NHL Draft. He figures he'd still be a first-rounder these days, but maybe his game would be dialled back a little: "It would have been a different game. I mean, I don't think I'd be throwing up 30-plus fights. Back then, that was the norm for a heavyweight. It's a different story in 2020."

Three and a half years after he was drafted, Mike Brown found himself in a Vancouver Canucks uniform in St. Louis, Missouri. Brown was traded to Vancouver in the Pavel Bure deal in January 1999. Brown was in St. Louis to play in his first NHL game. It didn't take him long to find a dance partner. Suited up for the Blues that night was his old WHL foe, Reed Low (one of the Blues' tough guys in the early 2000s). Mike Brown's first NHL fight came at the 2:26 mark of his second NHL period: "We knew each other from the summers. We kind of talked off the draw. I never really was one to say, 'Hey, you wanna go?' I sort of let things happen organically for the most part, unless it was necessary. I thought it might happen. Then we just started playing and then he elbowed me right in the face. He broke my nose, so it was on after that."

Brown and Low got five minutes each. In his first NHL game, Mike Brown had his first NHL fight. His first NHL goal, however, would have to wait: "The first fight was obviously way easier to get than the first goal. Back then, you probably had a choice of two or three guys to fight. If I touched the puck two or three times a game, that was great."

Patience would be a factor in Brown's chase for NHL goal number one. Right after that game against the Blues, Brown was sent back to the minors. While the rest of the Canucks boarded a plane for a game the next night in Washington, Brown had to catch up with his Kansas City Blades teammates, who were set to play the following night in Grand Rapids, Michigan. It was that quick: "It didn't kick in fully [that I had played in the NHL] until after the game, and then you're back with your regular team."

Fast-forward a couple of years later, and Mike Brown was now an Anaheim Mighty Duck. The Ducks claimed Brown on waivers on October 11, 2002. In Anaheim he found a GM that wanted him; his coach, not so much. "I got there and Mike Babcock basically said, 'Look, I don't need you. I don't want you. But Bryan Murray likes you. So I'm stuck with you for 30 days because of the waiver rules.'"

Babcock, Brown says, was true to his word. He spent 30 days with the Ducks and was then shipped off to the minors. But an injury to another Duck meant Brown got the call back up to Anaheim. And that brings us to a December night in Phoenix, just before Christmas in 2002. Mike Brown, a veteran of 22 NHL games, started the night with zero NHL goals. "I met with Babcock before the game and he told me I was like a cat with nine lives. He couldn't get rid of me. So I get in the lineup that night and scored. I mean, if I didn't score on that goal, I should have just hung them up. It was an awesome pass from Dan Bylsma. I kind of stuttered a bit and then I was like, 'Holy shit. I just scored in the NHL.'"

"We kind of cycled in behind the net. Jason Krog passed it out to Bylsma. Bylsma chipped it across the crease, and I did a hell of a job of burying it about two inches off the ice into the middle of the net. I probably could have turned my stick over and scored that goal, that's how nice the pass was."

Ten minutes later, Brown found himself in a more familiar role. Phoenix heavyweight Andrei Nazarov was on the ice as well. "Nazarov and I squared off. I was two-thirds of the way to a Gordie Howe hat trick in the first period."

He never did get there: "I don't know what happened after that. I guess I couldn't get that assist."

Brown scored a goal. Brown got into a tilt. He still could not figure out his head coach. "I played against his teams in junior, and I went after his guys. I did my thing. I think that kind of went into it. He'd call me in before practice and say, 'Hey, Brownie, you were an All-Star in junior and I've seen you play. You don't have to fight every shift. Work on getting some points and that sort of stuff.' And I'd say, 'Okay.' Then we'd go out and we'd win 3–1 or whatever, it would be a no-hitter, and then I'd get called in the next day and he'd say 'Brownie, what the fuck do you think you're here for? I got Hall of Famers in Oates and Kariya to score goals. You're here for one reason. You're the only guy that can do what you do in the organization.' So then I'd go out and pick a fight. I was so mind-fucked after that season."

Brown played 16 games for Babcock's Ducks. He finished with a goal, an assist, 44 PIMs and, as he stated, a bit of confusion. "I remember after I scored, I looked back at it, and I had a goal and an assist and five fights in seven games or something. And I was playing three minutes a game. For a fourth-liner, that's not bad. I was plus-1 or plus-2. I wasn't really costing us."

It didn't matter. Brown was not going to cut it with the Ducks. He spent the next few seasons bouncing around the minors. He played in his final two NHL games as a member of the Chicago Blackhawks, in 2005–06. By the end of that season, he was 27 years old. The game was changing: the first lockout was in the books and the salary cap was in effect. Being a 27-year-old minor-leaguer had its drawbacks. "I played one year after that lockout," says Brown. "You could see the transition from the 24-to-27-year-olds getting called up, because they had put in their time, to the entry-level guys getting called up. To be honest, mentally and physically, I was at the point where I said, 'Do I want to do this?' I was in really good shape to start the summer, but I decided 'No, I'm not feeling this. I should probably find a new career by 30 rather than by 40 when I'm really beat up.'"

First Round Brown was done. His NHL career was over. He ended his career with one NHL goal in 34 games. His 130 PIMs in those games are far more noticeable. But it's what is behind those 130 PIMs, that willingness to take a hit or take a punch for a teammate, that made Mike Brown the player that he was. You may think those 130 PIMs are just a number. They are not. They represent a great deal more: "I'm going to go out there, I'm going to bang. I'm going to be the guy that gets punched in the face instead of my linemate. That was just the way I was."

"I took pride in it. I was one of the bigger guys and I didn't like seeing my loved ones, my brothers, get hurt or get taken advantage of. And from a pretty young age I was pretty good at it. If someone was better than me at it, then you know what? Let's play rock-paper-scissors. I played with some tough, tough dudes, but I always thought I was the big dog on the team and it was on me to make sure that my guys were safe. Would I have liked to score more? Absolutely. There were times when I didn't really want to fight, but I'd rather do it than have somebody else do it. I'm glad I got one goal."

Mike Brown manages a GMC dealership in Vancouver these days. There are no reminders of his NHL past around the office. (The puck is on display in his father's house.) The only real reminders come via the odd email from his friends. "My buddies will send me a video every once in a while that they see online. It's pretty cool. It's definitely something I'm proud of. But hockey was one aspect of my life. There's a little more to me than just hockey. I think that goes for a lot of people out there."

"Hockey set me up for everything else [in life]. I got to be around the best and worst of people. And you just learn who you want to be as a person. That goal is cool. I'm super proud I did it. I'll pass my jerseys and sticks down to my kids. Yeah, your dad did this and that, but there's a lot of other stuff besides hockey, too."

CHAPTER NINE
JUNIOR STARS

KIMBI DANIELS

"Money on the board." Those are four magical words in the NHL. When a player returns to faceoff against an old team or the boys are in need of an extra boost, someone will usually put *money on the board*. In other words, they will offer cash to the player who scores the game winner that night. There was money on the board when the Philadelphia Flyers took on the Minnesota North Stars on October 24, 1991. "We had lost a few games. We didn't get off to a great start as a team. We started to feel a little bit of the pressure. I believe we had about $500 or so up on the board for the game winner. And Paul Holmgren was our coach. And he had Minnesota ties, so he matched it," says Kimbi Daniels.

The game was tied at 2 in the third when Daniels scored his first NHL goal. He says it was about as unlikely a goal as you'll ever see from him: "I was going down the wall and I ironically blistered a slapshot that went top shelf." Daniels says "ironically," since — he is the first to admit this — when it came to shooting, he was not quite Guy Lafleur. He was not known as a guy who just let one rip as he blazed down the wing: "My shot was never very hard. I very, very rarely took a slapshot. I guess I had a quick release and I always tried to hit the net no matter how soft the shot was. On a lot of teams I played on it was a running joke. Sometimes I would score from long range and the boys would say, 'Hey, how the hell did that go in?'"

But his shot against Jon Casey was hard enough and accurate enough to make Kimbi Daniels an NHL goal scorer. "I can count on one hand, in my junior and pro hockey career, how many times I scored a goal like that. For me it was just a low-percentage play, so I didn't like to make it. I don't think I could blow a shot by anybody, but in that case, to be honest, I didn't have time to get closer to the net. That's probably why I did shoot. It worked out."

The one question: Would the third goal of the night for the Flyers hold up as the game winner? It did. Philly skated off the ice at the end of the third with a 5–2 win. There was cash for Daniels: he earned it. "When we came in after the game, obviously I wasn't going to rip the money off the board. Everybody was saying, 'Who got the game winner? Who got the game winner?' I think it was Pelle Eklund who said, 'Kimbi got it.' He went and grabbed the money and brought it over to me. It was a nice little present for my first and only goal."

Daniels was a high-scoring centre with the Western Hockey League's Swift Current Broncos. He had 94 points in 69 games in his draft year. The Flyers took him with the 44th pick in the 1990 Draft. Daniels was already a Memorial Cup champ by that time. If you were a betting man, you would have wagered on Kimbi Daniels scoring a lot of goals in the NHL. But that fall at Flyers training camp, the Flyers doctors discovered very bad news: "When they did my X-ray during my first physical, they noticed something on my femur bone under my kneecap."

Daniels's knee was deteriorating. He kept playing. And the more he played, the worse his knee got. By the time his third Flyers camp came around, as he tells me, "The erosion had gone from the size of a dime to bigger than a quarter." Daniels had to make a decision. He had to do something about his deteriorating knee. If he kept playing like that, it would eventually wear down and maybe end his career. If the docs dug in and things went bad, that could also mean the end.

"It was tough. I was hoping that I'd be able to play again. The diagnosis that I got was to perform a bone graft. Their other suggestion was to cut a pie-wedge shape out of my shin bone and turn it around, to alleviate some of the pressure off of the middle part of my knee. And to me, that certainly wasn't an option. Just thinking about it makes me queasy, so I went with the bone graft."

"I don't think they had done it [before] at that point. They said if it worked, then maybe I could keep playing, or at least it would save the erosion on my knee. So I got the bone graft done and hoped for the best."

The procedure pretty much wiped out Daniels's entire 1992–93 season. He played in nine regular-season and another three playoff games for the WHL's Tri-City Americans. The following year, he managed to get in 48 minor league games, splitting time between the International and Colonial leagues. "Once I recovered, I found I could still skate and kind of do the things I had before. But I missed quite a bit of time. I don't think I ever regained my full speed."

"Prior to the injury, I played at a pretty high speed and was able to do stuff skill-wise, but I also was physical and could check. From that standpoint, it definitely [changed]. I noticed I became more of a defensive player after that. I was just trying to do things right and be on the right side of the puck. In hindsight, I probably should have just kept playing the way I did prior to my injury."

Kimbi Daniels, slowed down by an eroding knee, never made it back to the NHL. He scored his only goal when he was 19 and played in his final NHL game three days before his 20th birthday. "I was still pretty young [at the time of the operation], so I was thinking I can make it back to the NHL. Probably by the time I was 25, 26, I realized I wasn't going to play in the NHL again. But I really loved playing."

Daniels never did make it back to the NHL, but he never stopped playing pro hockey. He played until he was 35, mostly in the ECHL for the Alaska Aces. He still lives in Alaska today. "I just kept playing. I mean, what else would you rather do? There's just no substitute for it. And for me, having played in so many different places in the minors, they were all really, really good spots. There were so many places, playing in the IHL back then, it was a lot like playing in the NHL. You flew everywhere. You stayed in nice hotels in nice cities."

Salt Lake, Detroit, Baltimore, Saint Paul, New Orleans, Quebec City, and Phoenix are just a few of the cities where Kimbi Daniels suited up for the home side. The game was in Daniels's blood. It's not like he was struggling on the third line: in his last year as a pro, he led his ECHL's Phoenix RoadRunners in points. This is (very) rare in pro hockey. "During the last four years in Alaska and then the last year of my career in Phoenix, the game was actually becoming easier for me. It wasn't getting any harder. And I know the players were getting younger, they were getting faster, they were getting better, and I was thinking to myself, this has to end at some point. There has to be some slowdown and there wasn't. I just made the decision to stop playing and in hindsight I'm thinking, 'Geez, I probably could have squeezed out another two or three years.' Part of [my decision to retire] was the fact that the team in Phoenix folded. I know if they had kept going, I certainly would have played another year, because that place was fantastic to live in."

Daniels played his last professional game close to two decades after he scored his lone NHL goal. Once upon a time, Daniels scored all seven goals for his Swift Current Broncos in a 7–4 win over the Medicine Hat Tigers in 1990. Those seven goals in a single game are part of a WHL record he still holds with, among others, Ray Ferraro and Brian Propp. Daniels also won a Memorial Cup with the Broncos, and yes, he was there when the team was coached by Graham James.

"It's obviously a tough situation. Todd [Holt] and Sheldon [Kennedy], I love both of those guys. From a personal standpoint, it was the best place to play. There wasn't a bad thing about it. The biggest misconception is people think that everyone knew what was going on. That because we were a good team and we were winning a few hockey games that people turned a blind eye, and that certainly wasn't the case. The family I lived with, who Sheldon also lived with, if she had thought or they had felt that there was anything going on that was inappropriate, they would have put an end to it in a hurry. Even the people involved in the organization, they would have traded a good hockey team for stuff like that. I think that's the biggest misconception."

Kimbi Daniels's pro career lasted a long time and his junior days were a long time ago, but the abuse that happened in Swift Current will never be forgotten. The time that has transpired since then has made Sheldon Kennedy a household name. He is a child advocate now. Kennedy and Daniels were two of dozens of former Broncos who made it back to Swift Current for Hockey Day in Canada in the winter of 2019. Daniels found himself on an alumni team with a bunch of his old pals, including Kennedy, from his junior days. They sat just a few stalls from each other, both smiling and laughing and chirping one another, just like old hockey players do. "What Sheldon went through . . . I don't think he felt comfortable in Swift Current. But I think he's gotten past that. The city has helped him do that. For me as an individual and for other players that have played there, they have always spoke highly of it and enjoyed their time there."

And from Swift Current, it was on to the Philadelphia Flyers and that one goal against the North Stars. The night after that goal, Daniels and the Flyers were in Winnipeg for a game against the Jets. That was a big deal for a 19-year-old who was born a couple hours west of Winnipeg, in Brandon. Daniels had the chance to share his NHL life with his friends and family. "It may have been the longest 24 hours I ever had. I played the game, went out with some family after the game, and then hooked up with some of the guys at about 1 a.m."

Daniels, in that quick visit back to Winnipeg, had a lot of fun, but he also got to bring his friends and family into his new NHL world. That's a big deal: "I left home at 14 to play hockey, so I wasn't able to get really, really close with a lot of my siblings. I was always playing hockey, always gone, so that had a lot of meaning for me when I did get to see them, to be able to treat them to something like that. It was pretty nice. And I know they were always proud and appreciative just to say they had a brother who played in the NHL. That part of it makes me happy, for sure."

And the really good news was that Kimbi had plenty of cash, about $1,200, thanks to that money on the board from the night before, to show his family a good time. "Basically, the twelve hundred was gone less than 24 hours after I got it. But I treated my family well. We had a nice place to go eat. It was enjoyed, for sure. And not just by me."

JASON PODOLLAN

When 20-year-old Jason Podollan got the call to join the Florida Panthers in November of 1996, it was all just part of the plan. "I always thought that I was going to be a lifelong NHLer," he says. "That was sort of what was told to me. It was supposed to be in the cards. I just felt that that was just my destiny. I worked my tail off to get to where I was. When that call came, I was excited, but it wasn't like I was . . ." Podollan trails off, then continues: "You know when you think things are supposed to happen? There's a different feeling about it."

Less than two weeks later, the plan kept progressing. On a December night at the Spectrum in Philadelphia, Jason Podollan, who scored 145 regular-season goals for the WHL's Spokane Chiefs and who won World Junior gold for Team Canada in 1996, scored his first NHL goal. "It was a power-play goal on the rebound. Ray Sheppard was on the point. Jody Hull was on the half wall and put it to Sheppard at the point. He wristed one through and it came out to me in the mid slot, the hash marks, maybe a little bit tighter than that, and I put it through the goalie's legs. It wasn't pretty, but it went in."

"Never in my life would I have thought that would be my only goal. Never. I would have bet a million dollars there would be more."

But for NHL goals . . . that was it. Yes, he was in the NHL at just 20 years old; and yes, he scored a goal, but something just wasn't right: "I never did feel comfortable in an NHL jersey. The head-space scenario. I've gone over that now more in my late 30s and early 40s — when I was younger, in my 20s and even my early 30s, it was just something in my rear-view mirror. It's an interesting thing to be in an environment where you feel like you belong, and you feel like you're welcomed, and you feel like you're in a situation where people want you to succeed, as opposed to the other end of it. And you feel like you're on an island."

Podollan felt like he was the guy on an island. He was a kid on a team of men who had just willed themselves to the Stanley Cup Final the previous spring. He kept his mouth shut. He didn't ask questions. He tried to fit in: "I got a little bit of power-play time here and there. I was one of the guys on the periphery when I first got called up. And I didn't really find a groove where I thought, 'Okay, this is go time.'"

"I was a little bit star-struck. I didn't have enough time to be otherwise. I played against Wayne Gretzky and Mario Lemieux. I mean, Lemieux was my guy. He was my idol growing up."

All these years later, Podollan can clearly see his head was not in the right space. The feeling of not quite belonging affected Podollan's head. And when your head isn't right, chances are your game won't be either. "I wasn't able to slow my head down for the game. Everything was moving faster — and I was a fast player. I played fast. I was a strong skater. But I think I was in a scenario where I was thinking, 'Oh, my God. I gotta be this much faster and this much better!' And in doing that, the hamster was running a little bit faster than it needed to be. I needed to be able to slow the game down a little bit more. I was really worried about not making mistakes, as opposed to playing and getting comfortable."

Podollan never did find that comfort level in the NHL. Now, if there is anyone who can put his career in perspective, it is Jason Podollan. When he walked away from pro hockey at the age of 29, his final NHL stats read as follows: 41 games played, 1 goal, 5 assists, 6 points. These were not the totals he had dreamed of. "When I left pro hockey, I really thought of everything as a colossal failure, to be honest. I thought 'All right, this is done.' I mean, I enjoyed my career, but it was not anywhere close to what I imagined. I just sort of parked it."

Podollan, like a lot of other players, began searching for what he could do after hockey. He got into the beverage business, the restaurant business, and the golf business. But then he went back to his career. He started to think about his experiences in the game. Why was he the player he was? What could have been different? Now he helps people — men, women, young athletes — who are loaded with talent, but as Podollan says, "just don't have it figured out."

Podollan runs a company called Up My Life. He works with people who want to maximize their potential. "A lot of us think that we have it figured out, but we don't. For people to be able to lean on somebody that's been there, gone through it, didn't reach the realm of the NHL career that I wanted to . . . I can help these people precisely *because* I've been there; I've felt the pressure. It gives me real pleasure to be a resource now for other people. It's a great way to give back. And maybe my career happened for a reason."

Podollan is the type of person the 20-year-old version of himself never had the chance to talk to. "This is what I would tell the younger version of me: 'You know what you're supposed to be. You are destined to be there and you have to remember why you are there.'"

"There were so many things that might have helped me — mental preparation, for one. In the NHL now, what team *doesn't* have a psychologist on staff? Two, there is visualization or other tactics to slow the brain down. Three, meditation. When I was in the NHL, meditation was for a yogi somewhere on a mountain cliff. It was not even considered normal. But being able to channel your breath, to relate [to where you are] and to get into that self-awareness of where your emotions are, it's so powerful. If someone had been able to teach me some of those techniques, to step into the greatness, it would have been really powerful for me."

That's not to say Podollan is passing the buck. He knows he could have used some help when he was a 20-year-old hockey player, but he also knows, all these years later, that he could have done more: "I was a 20-year-old kid trying to figure it out and I kind of thought I did have it figured out. I take full responsibility. Other guys made it, in the same environment and conditions, but there wasn't much communication at all."

Here's another spot where the younger version of Podollan could use the wisdom of the older version. Just a few months after scoring that goal with the Panthers, Podollan was traded to the centre of the hockey universe. He was sent to the Toronto Maple Leafs in a one-for-one deal on March 18, 1997, for Kirk Muller. When a team trades away Kirk Muller, they obviously have high expectations for the kid they get in return. But the Leafs never told him any such thing. "It was a really weird scenario. Now looking back on it as a businessman, thinking about it — if I was the owner of that team or the GM or the coach, I'd be thinking: 'How do I want this 21-year-old guy to fit in on the team, what am I going to say to him? I mean, I want him to be great. We just traded for him. He's going to help our team. What can I do to get him off on the right foot?' In my case, none of that happened. It was a two-minute conversation. Just 'Welcome to the team, go get 'em.'"

"At 21 years old . . . I had a lot to figure out. Toronto is a tough spot to do that in if you play pro hockey. I wish that I was in a system where I felt I could be a little more vulnerable, where I could say, 'Hey, I'm really scared right now. I don't know anything about the city. I don't know anything about what I'm supposed to be doing. I don't know what my expectations are. I don't know what you guys want from me. I want to be the best I can, but I'm not sure how to figure it out.'"

Podollan did not say any of those things. In 1997 he did his best on a team that was not exactly great. The Leafs did not make the playoffs. Podollan finished the season in Toronto. He had three assists in 10 games. There was hope, however. The Leafs GM was Cliff Fletcher. He and Podollan had history. At the 1994 NHL Draft, Fletcher told Podollan that the Leafs were going to take him with their first-round pick. Podollan met with Fletcher for his interview the day before the draft. The meeting, in Podollan's mind, could not have gone better. Podollan says Fletcher told him the Leafs were going to trade up in the draft to make sure they could take him: "He shook my hand and he said, 'We'll see you tomorrow. You're going to be wearing a Maple Leafs jersey.' I walked out of that room on cloud nine. I thought, 'Holy shit. This is amazing.'"

The next day at the 1994 NHL Draft, things once again went according to plan for Podollan — at first. The Leafs, just like Fletcher had said they would, made a couple of trades and moved up. Toronto ended up with the 16th pick. "Then this weird thing happened. The mics [on the Leafs' draft table] came on and we definitely heard my name. My name came over the mic. But then they ended up picking [Eric] Fichaud. We were like, what the hell happened? After that, I didn't have a good feeling at all."

Podollan sat and waited for another 15 picks, until the Florida Panthers took him 31st overall. "That draft ended up being one of the worst days of my life. I had such big expectations. Leaving the floor, I got my Florida jersey on and I did my pictures. Walking out of the rink, Cliff Fletcher saw me and walked over. He put his hand on my shoulder and said, 'Jason, I just wanted you to know our head scout died before the draft. His guy was Fichaud. So we ended up going with his guy, in his memory. I'm sorry for that, but good luck with your career. You're going to be great.'"

A few years later, Podollan finally got the chance to play for Fletcher in Toronto. Podollan played 10 games with Fletcher's Leafs to finish the NHL season and then joined the AHL's St. John's Leafs for the playoffs. Podollan finally got a clear message at the end of the season: "Mike Murphy [Leafs head coach at the time] said at the end of the year that he wanted me to come back in better shape. I thought, 'All right, I'll blow the doors off this thing next year.'"

Podollan followed the coach's orders: "I was awarded the second-best-shaped guy in camp that year." And he lit it up in the pre-season. "I was the highest-scoring right winger in camp. I just felt like I was doing what needed to be done."

There was one problem. Cliff Fletcher was no longer the GM of the Toronto Maple Leafs. He was let go in May of 1997. That meant that Podollan had a new boss to impress. Think about any time you've had a new boss come in at work — inter-office politics are often at play. The hockey world is no different. "There wasn't anything I could do that was going to make any difference. I mean, how many goals does a guy need to score?"

"I was a Cliff Fletcher guy."

And that was pretty much it for Jason Podollan's NHL career. He scored 30 goals for the St. John's Maple Leafs in '97–'98. He scored 42 more — second in the AHL — the following year. He only managed to get into 12 more games (between the Leafs, Kings, and Islanders) in his NHL career. "After that, I never really got a chance and I couldn't really figure out why. Why wasn't that opportunity there again like I had in Toronto? But that's the window. You never know. But I did have the chance and I'll forever be thankful for that chance. It just didn't go the way I wanted it to. And I don't think I was really prepared for it when that chance was there."

Now Podollan wants to be there for kids just like him; kids that are maybe feeling that they aren't getting their proper shot. Right now he is working with, as he says, "civilians." He'd like to bring what he can offer to an NHL team: "I think there is a lot of opportunity there for help. To provide a service, so there's not someone on the end of a phone call with you saying, 'Shit, man, I had way more to give and I didn't give it.' I know there are a lot of guys out there who can benefit [from my experience]."

Jason Podollan does not think about his goal all that often. It did, however, help in shaping him into the person he is today. As he admits, when he quit pro hockey, he thought of his career as a colossal failure. But time has helped him put things in perspective. "Although it wasn't what I had planned, it is one goal more than a hell of a lot of other people out there have."

"I'm sure most guys, like me, who did make the NHL, even if only briefly, planned to score more than one goal. It's very nice that I got one and I can look at my trophy case right now and say, 'You know, that's pretty cool.' But I wanted there to be 499 more."

"Time gives perspective. I'm not that kid anymore. And I think I'm at a much healthier place with my career now. I'm in a position where I feel there is so much potential for me to help other people. I really do feel like I've found my calling now. Even more so than when I was a player."

CHAPTER TEN

A DIFFERENT PATH

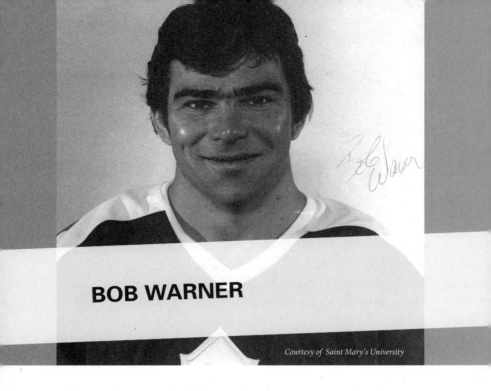

BOB WARNER

Courtesy of Saint Mary's University

When Bob Warner took his spot in line to sign up for classes at Saint Mary's University in Halifax in the fall of 1971, for the most part his dreams of an NHL career were over. Bob Warner was moving on: "I was fulfilling a dream of going to university and the possibility of one day becoming a teacher," begins Bob Warner. "I don't think anyone ever loses the desire to play in the NHL, but it really wasn't there anymore. It was time to buckle down and study and play hockey for Saint Mary's."

Warner arrived at Saint Mary's with one year of professional hockey under his belt. He spent the 1970–71 season with the Johnstown Jets of the old Eastern League. So, what was he doing in Halifax in the fall of '71? Well, a day before he enrolled at Saint Mary's, Warner was at camp with the Nova Scotia Voyageurs of the American Hockey League. He figured he would have been the sixth or seventh defenceman for the Halifax-based club. But at one point over that weekend, Vees coach Al MacNeil and Saint Mary's coach Bob Boucher had a chat. It was determined that

Warner would be better off going to Saint Mary's to play university hockey for the Huskies.

All these years later, not even Warner is sure who made the final decision to have him leave the Vees for the Huskies. Was it MacNeil, Boucher, or both? "I don't know. But knowing Bob Boucher and the kind of a guy that he was, and MacNeil, the type of coach that he was . . . they were always looking for an opportunity to bring in an undrafted guy, to see what he could do. The AHL was full of players who were drafted and had contracts. I didn't have one. Have you heard the term 'hiding somebody in the weeds?'"

That's what MacNeil wanted to do. Unlike in the AHL, Warner could get all the ice time he wanted in university hockey. And if he developed, then maybe Montreal could sign him down the road. The plan worked, in part: "My career at Saint Mary's took off. I was told a couple of times that Al MacNeil was at our games, but I never really had any more contact with them at all."

Warner was the backbone of a team that made it all the way to three national championship games. After his third year at SMU, the Montreal Canadiens didn't come calling. But another Original Six team did: he got an offer to attend Toronto Maple Leafs camp. Johnny Bower, whom Warner had met a few times over the years, invited him to try out for the Leafs. Warner politely declined. Following his fourth and final season, the future SMU Hall of Famer got another call from the Leafs. It was Bower again. Warner had fully planned on pursuing a career in teaching. He was 24 years old. The possibility of playing in the NHL wasn't on his radar, despite the call from Bower the year before. "My wife answered. She said, 'Johnny Bower's on the phone.' I said, 'Yeah, so is Mickey Mouse.' She insisted. So, I get on the phone. I said, 'Hello, Mr. Bower.' He said, 'Hi, Bob. It's John.'"

Warner's wife wasn't kidding. The Hall of Famer, a Leafs scout, was calling again. "I can honestly tell you I think my toes, everything, started to shake. I didn't know what was going to happen.

The next thing Johnny said was congratulations on this, this, and this. And then he said, 'We'd like to sign you to an amateur tryout, if that's okay?' I said, 'Of course it's okay!'"

Warner was over the moon. But he was still slightly grounded. Remember, he was 24 — in hockey terms, he was no spring chicken. Warner put his education to work. Before he ever stepped on the ice with the Leafs, he worked out a three-year deal with the team. Unlike a lot of invitees, Warner had a little bit of leverage — in the form of that degree from SMU. "What they offered was low league, it was minor league money. My comeback to them, simply put, was 'I can make a whole lot more money than that teaching.' It was pretty ballsy on my end, I'll admit that, but I had something in my hand I had worked for: my degree. I wasn't going to not take advantage of it."

Warner signed his deal before he went to camp. He even got a signing bonus: "I was able to pay off my student loan. It was pretty sweet." In his first year with the Leafs organization, Warner managed to get into a couple of playoff games. He had to wait almost a full calendar year for another taste of the NHL. He was called up in late February of 1977. In the ninth game of his 10 game tenure with the Leafs, Bob Warner found the back of the net against the Colorado Rockies in Denver. "I was getting a lot more chances with the puck than I normally did. I felt comfortable. I was not intimidated. I had a lot of close calls before I scored, a couple of close shots. It was a line change."

Just under seven and a half minutes into the first period, the Leafs were on the forecheck. The puck eventually found its way to Warner. "Do I remember where I put the puck? No. It was one of those rebounds out in the slot. I skated for the puck and wheeled around, and I just slapped it. The next thing I knew, it was in the net and all hell broke loose. I think I was jumping up and down like a wild man. It happened so quickly."

Bob Warner was an NHL goal scorer. He had encountered some hockey legends in his time: Stanley Cup–winning coach Al

MacNeil; university legend Bob Boucher; Hall of Famer Johnny Bower. But it was a lesson he got from an old peewee coach that really paid off in Denver: "I can always remember my peewee coach, Mr. Belanger. He would say in his great French accent, 'Shoot that puck! Shoot that puck!' I can honestly still remember it. I would think, 'Shoot the puck. Don't do anything with it. Shoot the puck.' I wheeled and I pivoted. I got good wood on it. I was told afterwards it was stick side and it went straight in."

Lanny McDonald grabbed the puck. He handed it to the trainer. The moment stayed with Warner, but the puck seemed to disappear. "I went to camp the next fall. On the second or third day, Johnny Bower came over. He said, 'You're having a great camp. The coaches would like to see you for a second.'" Like any player on the bubble, Warner thought the worst: "Aw, where am I going? Saginaw? I don't know."

Bob Warner headed into the office. Bower was in there. The coaches were in there. A few scouts were there as well: "They had this silver-cased plaque. They mounted the puck for me. I had completely forgotten about the puck. After that game when I scored, I asked the trainer who had the puck. He told me, 'Don't worry. It's taken care of.' Eventually I kind of forgot about it. It's just a puck. But the Leafs mounted the puck on a beautiful plaque. It said: 'Bob Warner. First NHL goal March 16, 1977. Toronto 4 – Colorado 4.' It's the old Rockies puck. It might be worth some money now."

Camp went along well for Warner until he got caught up in a numbers game. The Leafs had a lot of young picks coming into camp. He ended up in the Central League with Dallas in 1977–78. After two more years in the American League, Warner retired from professional hockey. "For what started out as a journey for me to go to school, I ended up getting five years of [pro hockey after university], which is not bad. I can say I was there. I saw some action. I figured out I would see what I could do with my degree."

Warner planned on becoming a teacher. Instead, his career took a turn and he went into sales and marketing. He worked for Hershey for a number of years. He's back in Halifax now, where he took that turn from the Vees to Saint Mary's and where the adventure all began: "It was really one of the more roundabout ways to make the NHL."

STEVE COATES

When Steve Coates wrapped up his four-year career at Michigan Tech, he was looking for something, anything, or anyone that would let him break into the professional hockey ranks: "I couldn't even get my college coach to get me into a pro tryout," says the Philadelphia Flyers broadcaster.

Like a lot of college graduates, Steve Coates just needed an in. When you get out of college you take any break you can get, whether you're trying to get into the business world or the hockey world. Soon enough, Steve Coates got his break courtesy of the Philadelphia Flyers: "I came here to Philadelphia in '73 because a gentleman named Alex Davidson was the chief scout at the time and I had played with his son Brad, in Markham. So I called him and I said, 'I'm just looking for an opportunity to go to training camp.' He said no problem, and I came to Philly."

A chance was all Steve Coates wanted, and that's what the Flyers organization gave him. When camp opened, he knew where he stood; or, rather, where he sat. The Flyers and the players from their Richmond AHL affiliate were on one side of the rink. Coates and the rest of the amateurs were in another room on the other side of the rink. "It was basically a class society. You were a free agent, and that's the way you were treated."

Coates did enough to earn a job in the International League with the Des Moines Capitals. He averaged almost a point a game in his first pro season. He had 70 points in 72 games and finished second on the team with 167 PIMs. His team won the league title. He was signed the next year to go to Richmond of the AHL. He spent the next three seasons in the Flyers' minor league system, playing in the American Hockey League until he was traded as part of a five-player deal to the Detroit Red Wings on February 7, 1977: "I certainly wasn't a big part of the trade. I was the 'and' in the trade."

But when the Wings made the deal, they had no plans to keep Coates in the AHL. He joined the big club right away. Just like that, after four seasons slugging it out in the minors, he was an NHLer. There was just one problem: "It was a hard time for me when I got traded. I had a pulled groin when I got there [to Detroit]. I played the first game against Buffalo."

Coates was an NHLer. "I was excited, but the thought of that pulled groin was first and foremost on my mind. I was worried that I was going there and I was hurt. But in those days, you didn't tell anybody unless you couldn't walk. And that's what I had. I had a problem where I could not play the way I should play with the pulled groin."

He sucked it up. But by his second game with the Wings, his groin had had enough. It set up perhaps the only dump-and-chase, or make that dump, on a breakaway, in the history of pro hockey: "I blocked a Bert Marshall shot in our zone and the puck went back into the neutral zone and I had a breakaway. I forgot about my groin."

In a flash, Coates's injury woes had disappeared, maybe not physically, but at least mentally. The only thing between him and his first NHL goal was Islanders goaltender Chico Resch. "I went from the blue line to the red line. I got to the red line and my groin absolutely snapped. I got to the far blue line and I couldn't skate anymore, so I fired the puck into the corner and skated right to the bench. The crowd went from 'Yeah!' to '*Boo!*' in the same breath." At least Coates got the puck in deep. "To this day, everybody says at least you're coachable; you dumped it in."

There was no need for Coates to tell the Red Wings he couldn't play anymore. They could see it. His groin was shot. Coates was on the shelf for three weeks. This was 1977, so the NHL wasn't exactly on the cutting edge of high-performance training, injury prevention, or recovery, for that matter. "When I played, we didn't stretch like the players do today, so groins were a really common problem. To be honest . . . 40 years ago, the only thing that was good for a groin was rest."

Coates sat for 28 days. He returned to the lineup on March 28. A few days later, he was in the Wings' lineup for the fourth game of his NHL career; that night, Detroit played the Pittsburgh Penguins. It was a special night for Steve Coates. His dad, John, and his uncle made the drive down from Toronto. For the first time ever, John Coates sat in the stands and watched his son play in an NHL game. The first thing Steve did to impress the old man that night, 26 seconds into the game, was drop the gloves with Russ Anderson. What came next was much better. "The puck was in the corner to the left of [Pittsburgh goaltender] Denis Herron. Dennis Polonich had it in the corner, got it out front, and I just fired it. It went over the right shoulder of Herron."

Steve Coates was an NHL goal scorer. Did he think it would happen? "No, sir. I was a so-so college player. But my dad was there when I scored my NHL goal: you couldn't write a script better than that. I played five games in the NHL, and to have him come down and be there when I did it, I mean . . . that meant everything in the whole world. It was something special — to have my dad come for my fourth game in the National Hockey League and have me score. That's something that will remain with me forever."

Steve Coates and his father didn't have one of those magical *Field of Dreams* moments after the game. You know, the kind of moment where father and son just look at one another, without saying a word, but knowing that something special had just happened. "We went and drank beer." And yes, if you're wondering, Steve picked up the tab. When he went from the minors to the NHL his salary doubled from $17,500 to $35,000 a year: "I was living the life then."

Steve Coates only had one more NHL game left in his career to live large on that salary. After another three years in the minors, he retired. Just like after his college career came to an end, he got another break after his pro career. Philadelphia Flyers owner Ed Snider was expanding into the strange new world of cable TV and he needed some talent in front of the camera and on the microphone. Coates had a bit of the broadcasting bug: "I stayed in Philadelphia during the summers and I used to imitate broadcasters. I've always been a guy to tell jokes and things like that."

So, when Snider started PRISM Cable and took a number of broadcasters to the TV side, the Flyers needed some help on the radio for 30 home games on WIP radio. Enter the funny hockey player who used to imitate the announcers: "They gave me the opportunity because it was 30 games. I didn't have to travel, and that's how I started."

Like any new broadcaster, Coates went through some growing pains. He says it took him a long time to find his voice. "Most hockey players, I find, come in and think 'Well, I'm a pro hockey player. I'll just go on and talk.' I was like that. A guy named Pete Silverman helped me out. Sat with me and made me understand what I had to do."

Coates did four years of radio. When the 1984–85 season rolled around, Coates was informed he'd be doing a pre-game coaches' show on TV. He had never been in a TV studio. Two weeks later, he was in a TV studio hosting a TV show for the first time. "I was absolutely a mess." Coates made his way through show number one. When it came time to say so long, he was pretty nervous: "By accident, I even thanked myself for being on the show."

So far, so good. Gene Hart's signature sign off was "Good night and good hockey." Coates figured he'd say the same thing. But instead of saying, "Good night and good hockey," Coates looked into the camera and uttered, "Good night, good evening." Now, that's a minor and almost unnoticeable flub for a viewer. But for a green young broadcaster, that can feel like the end of the world. "The producers . . . well, I don't want to tell you what the producers said."

It was time to get Steve Coates up to TV snuff. He met with (of all people) Ronald Reagan's speech coach. That's a pretty high-ranking tutor. "I spent four hours with him." Those four hours have helped Coates sail along on a broadcasting career that has lasted almost four decades. With the exception of the 1991–92 season and a chunk of the '92–'93 season, he has been a constant on Flyers broadcasts, whether they were on TV or radio. That one goal has given him a great run: "I don't know if it's the goal or my mouth," laughs Coates.

So, where does that goal rank in a hockey life that has seen him crack an NHL roster, broadcast hundreds of NHL games, and even play Santa Claus for the Flyers on TV? (It's worth looking up on YouTube.) "I don't think the goal can be first, just because it was a one-moment thing. It's obviously important for your own peace of mind that you did score a goal in the National Hockey League. It's something special. Like you said earlier, there's a lot of guys who didn't [do it], and I never dreamt that I would be there. So, for me to have that happen, it's something special. Where it ranks . . . I don't know how to compare it against being a broadcaster for a National Hockey League team for 37 years, after only having played five games in the National Hockey League. So, it's really hard to make that comparison. The career I've had here is unbelievable. But that one goal, at least you can say, 'I did it.' I joked on a broadcast the other night, maybe it was Crosby, I think he's at around 450. I said he's only got 449 more than me."

HANK LAMMENS

There's an interesting little gap on Hank Lammens's hockey stat line: the 1991–92 season does not exist. It does not exist because Lammens had other things on his mind: specifically, the 1992 Olympics; that is, the 1992 Summer Olympics. The professional hockey player put down his skates and jumped into his sailboat: "Looking back at it now, in the summers I spent too much time sailing, and in the winter I spent too much time playing hockey. The way guys do sports now is definitely not the same model, but I couldn't have done it any other way," says former Olympic sailor — and NHL goal scorer — Hank Lammens.

Sailing and hockey had been on equal ground for Lammens since he was a kid growing up in Brockville, Ontario. Brockville just happened to be the main training site for Canada's national sailing team. Most kids these days, those who actually play multiple sports, usually have a decision to make by their mid-teens. Which sport do I concentrate on? Lammens just kept on doing both; it was a world-class juggling act.

"During my first year of junior hockey, I missed training camp because I was at the World Sailing Championships in Italy. I came back from Italy and I missed camp, but I made the team. The next year, I had qualified for the Worlds, which were in Auckland, New Zealand, in December. And that was my college hockey-recruiting year. I said to the coach: 'I qualified for the Worlds. I'm the only guy in Canada who qualified. Would it be okay if I miss a couple of weeks of hockey in December?' I was the team captain. My coach said, 'Absolutely. You go.' So I missed a couple of games in December because I was at the World Sailing Championships in New Zealand, which was a great experience."

Lammens says this all very casually. He was competing on the world stage in sailing and also playing good enough hockey to earn a scholarship to St. Lawrence University. While he was at school he kept up both sports, sailing in the summer and hockey in the winter. He was good enough on the ice to be drafted by the New York Islanders in 1985 and was eventually named an all-American with St. Lawrence. "The year that I was selected an all-American was pretty cool. My partner on the plaque was a guy named Brian Leetch."

Lammens was keeping world-class company on the ice and on the water. He started his pro hockey career in 1988 with the Springfield Indians and kept on sailing in the summer. A couple of years later, while he was still in the American League, Lammens struck gold on the water. He won his first World Sailing Championship in 1990 followed by another one in 1991. Even though it may not have been a big deal for the Canadian media at the time, Canada had a real two-sport star. "A lot of people don't understand what international sailing in the Men's Heavyweight Finn Class is. I won the Worlds in 1990 in Greece. Then I went to visit my sister, who lived in Portugal at the time. When I got to her town, they gave me the key to the city. I was named a lifetime member of the yacht club there. It was a huge deal. To be a Finn Cup Gold champion is huge in Europe. Then when I came home to Canada, my yacht club had a little thing, they put out a sign in front, and that was about it. People really didn't understand what it was that I accomplished."

Lammens was a world champ, but he was not mobbed on the streets in Canada. He was, however, nominated for Canadian Athlete of the Year in 1991. He lost to Kurt Browning. "I went to this big thing. It was the sailor and the figure skater. When I got called up to the podium people seemed to think, 'All right, cool.' When he was up there, it was like we were at a Beatles concert. So, the sailor isn't going to win that," Lammens says with a chuckle.

He was treated like a Stanley Cup champ in Europe, but not quite at home. And with the 1991–92 season approaching, Lammens decided to put his pro hockey and Stanley Cup dreams aside. He stepped away from professional hockey that season to prepare for the Barcelona Olympics. Lammens finished 13th in Barcelona. When he came home, he had to figure out what was next. He had no idea. His brainstorming session lasted about 24 hours: "I got back from Barcelona and I sat at home for a day or so. And all of a sudden, the phone rang and it was Paul Henry, who was the GM of the Canadian national team."

Yep, Lammens was about to hit the ice again. And another Olympics was in sight — the 1994 Winter Olympics in Lillehammer, Norway. "Henry said, 'Knowing you, I think you'll be the captain of the team and you can compete in the summer and winter Olympics.' I thought, 'That sounds good.' He asked me to think about it. I asked when he needed me in Calgary. He told me, 'Camp starts in two weeks.' I said, 'Well, can I come out on Monday? Because I have to skate.' I hadn't skated in a year."

Lammens loaded up his truck and made the drive to Calgary. The plan was now in place. Hank Lammens, summer Olympian, was set to become Hank Lammens, winter Olympian. But plans do change. Paul Henry was half right: Lammens did captain the team, but he didn't stick around for the Olympics. "I got an opportunity to sign with Ottawa. I thought . . . the National Hockey League is pretty good."

And that is how the Olympic sailor became the NHL goal scorer. Lammens spent most of the 1993–94 season with PEI in the AHL, but he did play in 27 games with Ottawa, including a game on November 27, 1993, at the old Igloo in Pittsburgh. "Last summer, I was there with a kids' team for a hockey tournament. We were playing in the Penguins' new rink. I pointed to the parking lot and I told the kids, 'That's where I scored my goal. They tore down the Igloo.' And all the kids said, 'What are you talking about?'"

"The goal was kind of a new-era goal. I followed up on the play. I was the trailer. We were on a three-on-two. Alexei Yashin had the puck down the wall. I think the defenceman looked at me and thought, 'Well, that guy's not going to get the puck.' Yashin dropped it back. I shot it far corner, along the ice. Maybe the goalie thought I was going to dump it in or something."

So, the world champion and Olympic sailor was now an NHL sniper. Hank Lammens has a pretty nice resumé. It is padded out with his current gig, working in the financial district in New York City. "The Gold Cups obviously were, for me, the peak in sailing, and for me, in hockey, the year I was selected as an all-American is up there," Lammens says when he's asked to rank where his goal fits into his journey. "Hockey-wise, to be recognized over a full season was pretty cool. Scoring that goal is not really something I focus on."

Just how casual is Hank Lammens about his lone NHL goal? Very. Exhibit A: "My son was starting to skate. He was three or four years old. We have a little pond in the backyard. He started skating around and I got him a little stick. I hadn't really skated in a long time because I was trying to do this Wall Street thing. We were skating around and we needed a puck. I remember I had two pucks on my workbench. One puck was the one from my first goal at St. Lawrence and the other one was the puck from my goal in Pittsburgh. I went and got them, and my son and I started to pass one of the pucks around. There was a little open ice where the water was flowing in. I passed the puck to my son and he missed it. So, the puck goes into the bog and I was down to one puck."

Breathe easy, everyone, there is nothing to worry about. It was the St. Lawrence puck — hold on . . . wait. Exhibit B: "About 20 minutes later, we lost the other puck. So I lost both of my sentimental pucks. They're actually still out there somewhere in my backyard in this mud bog. They're gone."

CHAPTER ELEVEN

HIGHER EDUCATION

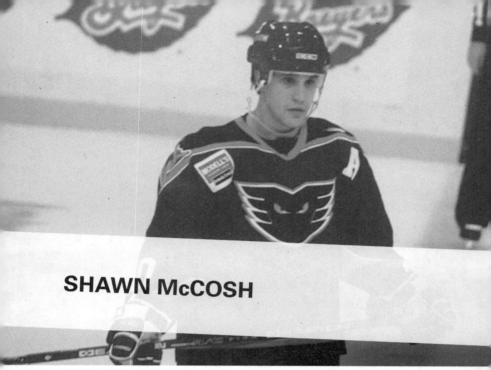

SHAWN McCOSH

One of the great things about being a kid and going to school was hearing about the teachers you would encounter in the years to come. Maybe an older brother or older friend would warn you about how strict the junior high gym teacher is or how hard Mr. X's grade seven English class is. In a middle school in the Phoenix, Arizona, area these days there is a story about Mr. McCosh. The story goes like this: "My teacher, Mr. McCosh, can take his teeth in or out!" says Shawn McCosh.

Former NHLer Shawn McCosh is indeed the very same Mr. McCosh. He teaches grade seven social studies. Once upon a time, a very long time ago, back on February 1, 1995, Mr. McCosh scored goal for the New York Rangers. That has to be a huge deal for his students, right? "I live in Arizona. Hockey's getting popular down here, but there are other things that interest the kids. They're not playing road hockey and ice hockey like we did all year round."

Still, you have to think it's pretty cool that your teacher once sniped for the Blueshirts, even if you're a kid in the desert. You hear of a ton about players who find a new life away from the game once they retire. Not everyone becomes a coach or a scout or a broadcaster. Many others become financial advisors, real estate agents, or business owners. What you don't often see are former NHLers who become middle school teachers. "I enjoyed school when I was a kid. I enjoyed learning. I think when I had my kids, my first daughter, I enjoyed being a parent and teaching and helping her. I think that teaching is probably something that was in me."

During a pro career that took him from New Haven to LA to Binghamton and New York, as well as many other stops along the way, Shawn McCosh remembered to keep the books within reach. He took college courses on the side. He'd slip in a few during the summer. We may think that pro hockey players do nothing but hang out on the lake and the golf course during the off-season; that was not entirely the case for McCosh. "I always thought that if you're not using your brain and you're sitting around and you're not doing anything [it's not going to help you]. I was just trying to grow academically all the time. Not that it's a bad thing if you sit and relax and have some time off, but I knew I wanted to keep challenging myself."

During his fifth season as a pro, McCosh got his second-ever call-up to the NHL. (His first one was with the LA Kings for a four-game stint in 1992.) This time, he got the call to join the New York Rangers. The Rangers were coming off their famous 1994 Stanley Cup win, but they, and the rest of the NHL, had to wait until late January of 1995 to start the next season thanks to a labour dispute. In his second game with the club, McCosh, once a 103-point man in the OHL, scored the Rangers' second goal of the game 7:11 into the third in Pittsburgh. The goal tied the tilt 2–2. "The puck went around the boards. Joey Kocur threw it back to Kevin Lowe on the point. I just went to the net. I remember thinking, 'Get the puck to the net. Get the puck to the net.'"

That is exactly what Lowe did. McCosh did the rest: "I deflected it in the net. Kocur and Lowe made me feel really good about scoring my first goal. Joey was great to me. He was really good about it."

Another guy was pretty pumped about the goal, too. It was Ron McCosh, who caught the highlights that night. "Dad told me he was watching the highlights of the game and saw the goal. He said he jumped off the couch. Dad used to stay up and watch the highlights when I got called up, so that was kind of neat when Dad called me after the game."

"My dad was always supportive of me. The lessons he taught me: be accountable and work hard. The only thing he would say to me is: 'I don't care if you're the worst player or the best player in minor hockey, but I get up in the morning to take you to hockey, so I expect you to work hard.'"

After another week and a half with the Rangers, it was back to the minors. That work ethic his father instilled served him well. McCosh played pro for anther five seasons. He's just as proud of hanging around and being a pro until he was 31 as he is of scoring in the NHL. And he also figures he caught a bit of the teaching bug during his final few years as a pro. "When I was playing in the AHL in Philadelphia, one of my roles as an older player at the time — I was 27, 28 — was to be a good team player and help the younger kids, the prospects who were coming up. I was there to show them the professional side of the game and to help then get better so they could move on."

"It's funny, you don't really think about what you're accomplishing as a player when you're in the moment. But once you're done you look back at where you were and who you played with. One of the things I'm most proud of: I played a lot of my career in the minors. Trust me when I say that is not easy. I played right up until I was 30-plus years old; to do that you have to be a good character person. You have to be a person who brings value to an organization. You help the kids. You have to be a good person to have around. I think playing a lot of years in the minors is tough. When I look back on it, I think, 'Holy cow! That was long.' The stuff that I went through, even to just get called up to the NHL and play, you're kind of proud of what you did. But you don't think of your accomplishments at the time."

"I definitely had some breaks. I was a decent player and I got some good breaks. I think there were times — actually, I bet most hockey players might say this — there were times when I could have went the other way and been cut, or not had the opportunities I did and my whole life would have changed. I was fortunate to have some people who stuck with me and liked me and gave me opportunities. I think that's one of the things I think about the most, when I think about playing at that level and playing for as long as I did . . . and where I did."

Within a couple of years of retiring, McCosh had his degree. It was time to find a teaching job. That night he scored for the Rangers, his shooting percentage was 100. He had one shot on the Pens and he scored. He was about to do the same thing as a would-be teacher: "I went to my very first interview and they hired me right away. At the end of the interview, they took me around the school and showed me everything. I thought, 'This is kind of interesting. Is there usually a tour of the school after a first interview?' Before I was even home, I got a call and they said, 'Would you like to accept the job?'"

McCosh took the gig. He figured that was pretty easy. He eventually asked his new principal: Is it just me, or was this too easy? It was a little strange to McCosh that he got the gig so easily. Turns out, all that life experience McCosh had, the fact that he wasn't just a young kid fresh out of a school, was one of the deciding factors. Apparently all those hours on the bus in the minors paid off: "They told me I had some real-life experiences that were going to help me in the classroom. And to be honest, I think my principal was right. I have used a lot of ups and downs and situations that I learned in hockey, to help me in the classroom, and I think those ups and downs have helped me be a better teacher."

I can't imagine there are many similarities between life in the NHL and teaching 11- and 12-year-olds. McCosh played with genuine hockey royalty — Mark Messier in NY and Wayne Gretzky in LA. At the end of his hockey career, McCosh got to teach young players about what it was like to be a pro. Now he gets to teach young kids about history and government. That's range. So, is he a better teacher or a better hockey player? "Oh, that's a good one. I'll say the thing I'm most proud about is that I try to be a pro in everything I do. I feel like I was a good pro when I played, meaning I was a good team player, a guy who if things went really wrong, that I was still a good person and a guy who wanted to help the team win. So I try to do that as a teacher. I've found that I still have a lot of things to learn about teaching and the kids are changing, so you have to adapt to all that stuff. I would say I'm still learning in teaching, but I'm coaching now in hockey. And I'm still learning in that, too."

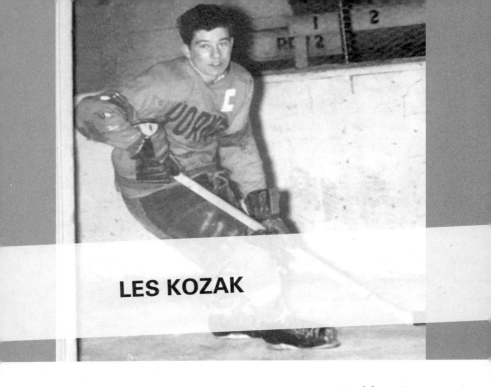

LES KOZAK

The priesthood. Your first pro contract. Your NHL debut. Your first NHL goal. A devastating head injury. Normally, that's a lifetime. For Les Kozak, it was a few months. The St. Mike's Majors, coached by the legendary Father David Bauer, won the 1961 Memorial Cup without Les Kozak. Kozak had passed on his final year of junior eligibility to attend a monastery. The hockey prospect decided to become a priest. "After eight months, I decided it wasn't for me and I returned [to St. Mike's]," he recalls.

By that time, it was too late for Kozak to join his old teammates on the ice. St. Mike's defeated the Edmonton Oil Kings in early May of 1961 to win the championship without him. But he had done enough from his play in previous years to get a contract from the Maple Leafs. Kozak signed and then started his professional career with the AHL's Rochester Americans in the fall of 1961. One night that season, Punch Imlach made the trip to Rochester to scout his farm club. "He had an injury to one of his players and needed to bring someone up from the Rochester Americans. That was a Friday night, the 12th of January. He came into the dressing room after the game. I did well that game: I scored two goals." Kozak got the news that he was headed to Toronto.

Kozak's childhood prayers were answered. He put on a Leafs jersey for the first time and played for the team he'd dreamed of playing for as a boy. But he was anything but intimidated on the Gardens ice that night: "I felt pretty comfortable going from Rochester to Toronto that Saturday morning before the game. Bear in mind that when I was at St. Mike's, we did our regular practices at Maple Leaf Gardens and we played our games at Maple Leaf Gardens. I was very comfortable in that environment. I had been used to hearing the national anthem being played before the game. But of course, it was nothing like the experience when I was with the Leafs."

To make things even more comfy for Kozak that night, he was playing with not only one of his old teammates but one of his old St. Mike's roommates as well. He was on a line with Dave Keon and legendary Leaf George Armstrong. At the 6:46 mark of the third, things clicked for the trio: "I went around Marcel Pronovost enough to get a clear shot, and I was actually surprised it went in," Kozak chuckles. "In those days, you never got pumped up like they do today when you scored a goal. We were all rather subdued and we didn't show our emotions at all. But I got back to the bench after the goal and George Armstrong handed me the puck." The goal tied the game at 3–3. The Leafs went on to beat Detroit 4–3 that night.

Kozak may not have shown much emotion after that goal, but he was thrilled: "I think the biggest emotion was satisfaction, the personal satisfaction, that I had become successful in something that was a dream for much of my life. I think that was the strongest emotion that I had."

And then there are the little things that Kozak remembers from that night, other than the goal. The fact that he knew a lot of the usherettes at the Gardens, that he had friends in the stands, and even a simple thing like a note that was waiting for him after the game: "A really big memory of that night was that when I got back to the dressing room, there was a telegram there from my grade one teacher." Everyone was excited for their friend Les Kozak. And so was he.

One game into his NHL career and Les Kozak already had his first NHL goal. He stuck with the Maple Leafs and got to play in 11 more games. He played in every Original Six barn with the exception of New York. Those magical old pictures you see of the Montreal Forum where the fans are practically on top of the players? Kozak lived it: "There was such a contrast between the brilliance of the colours of the uniforms and the brilliance of the ice and the crowd. You couldn't distinguish people [in the crowd]. It was just a mass of charcoal-coloured bodies, and what would strike me, was that when there was an occasion for them to cheer, it would be like an eruption. And you just couldn't [distinguish them], because they were so densely packed in. They were all in their dark-coloured winter clothes. I never forgot that. That memory struck me."

And then there was Detroit and playing against Gordie Howe, who was a hero for thousands of Canadian kids, including Kozak. "I remember being manhandled by him in the corner one game. I don't recall showing too much respect for him, but he knocked me around in order to teach the young kid a lesson or two."

When his cameo with Toronto came to an end, Kozak headed back to Rochester. His first season of pro was going along swimmingly, until his career, and almost his life, came to an end in Providence, Rhode Island, on February 23, 1962. "It was in the first period. I was trying to make an impression on some people in the rink and I let my guard down. I was a little foolish to try to get between Fern Flaman and the boards to try to get a puck that would have given me a breakaway. I was playing the puck, and he played me. He hit me pretty hard and my head hit a metal post that was used to keep up a screen that protected the fans from the pucks. I fell to the ice."

Kozak was dazed and bleeding, not all that unusual for that time. He was taken to the medical room and stitched up. He eventually made his way back to the Americans dressing room and lay down on a bench. When his teammates headed out to the ice for the second period, Kozak didn't move. By the time the third period rolled around, Kozak was still lying on the bench. That's when he noticed something: "My head started bothering me and I felt a little numbness in my left hand."

An ambulance was called, but it didn't make it to the rink before the game was over. By the time the Americans were ready to board their bus, Kozak was still with them. Years later, he learned what exactly went down in the moments before the Americans boarded their bus to head back home. "I understand from a report from Terry O'Malley, who I was very close to at St. Michael's, that he had talked to Bruce Draper, who was on our Rochester team. Bruce told him that when the coach or management wanted to take me back to Rochester on the bus, the players insisted, especially Dick Gamble, that I be taken to the hospital." Gamble and the rest of Kozak's teammates stood their ground. Kozak was loaded into an ambulance. "I remember a very bumpy, painful ride to the hospital in an ambulance and then being asked to sign some release documents for surgery to be done on me."

Kozak had a depressed fracture in his skull. In layman's terms, his skull was broken. He was rushed into surgery. He woke up hours later, with little or no clue of what had happened. "The next thing I remember, of course, is waking up the next morning. I don't recall feeling bad or having any headache or anything like that." There was a noticeable effect of the surgery. "Ever since then, I've been walking around with a hole in my head the size of a golf ball."

When Kozak was eventually released from the hospital he stayed with his fiancée, who happened to be living in Providence, for 10 days. He then made his way up to Boston when the Leafs visited the Bruins. He flew back with the Leafs to Toronto. Kozak, who was attending college at the time, and expected his hockey career to be a brief one anyway, before he went to school full time, had no intention of playing anymore. He was checked out by the Toronto brass and made his way back to Rochester, where he picked up on courses he had been taking at St. John Fisher College. That May, while he was in Rochester, Kozak says he became very ill: "I had a serious bout with Dilantin [a seizure medication] toxicity. I got very sick. A neurologist at Rochester Medical School told me that I should not play hockey again."

Kozak knew that news was coming, but now it was official — no more hockey. "It was earth-shattering . . . just shattering. I had been dreaming of being a Leaf forever."

He got married that June back in Toronto and planned to continue with his studies. There was just one problem. The Leafs wanted him to play at training camp that fall. Kozak was armed with the Rochester doctor's report and did not attend camp. That November, he underwent another surgery; and all the while, the Leafs were waiting for him to suit up again. "They repaired the hole in my head. Bear in mind, they expected me to play *even though I had a hole in my head.*"

During all of this, Kozak was still attending school, and he was a very able student. But the mental effects of his injury began to emerge. In an era well before society openly talked about mental illness, Kozak fell into a deep depression: "I was still at St. John Fisher College, a year or so after the injury. It was a difficult time. There's a response you have every fall — when you can play hockey all your life, you expect to do that. And, of course, I couldn't; so, a combination of that, plus the lack of confidence that develops when you have a head injury like that, caused me to go through periods of depression. I was able to overcome it basically due to the support of my wife and the fact that by then, we had children as well."

Two or three years later, now well-removed from the game, Kozak found his true calling. It was not in a church. It was not on the ice. It was in a lab. "For the longest time, I got involved in a rather demanding course of study. I decided to become a chemist and study chemistry and biology as an undergraduate, and then I had grades good enough to get a fellowship to the University of Notre Dame in chemistry. While I was there I became interested in biochemistry and subsequently molecular biology; and being a molecular biologist has been the course of the rest of my life."

Dr. Les Kozak spent decades working at the Jackson Laboratory in Bar Harbor, Maine. He has been a faculty member at Louisiana State University and a professor at the Institute of Animal Reproduction and Food Research of the Polish Academy of Sciences in Olsztyn, Poland. That's a long way from a goal assisted by Dave Keon and George Armstrong in 1962 and that career-ending injury close to six decades ago. "How did they [those moments] affect the rest of my life? Wow." Dr. Kozak takes a long pause. "That's a tough question to answer. I don't know if they made any significant change in the rest of my life. I can't say that certainly. I had expected that I would not play hockey very long — that I would play a few years of hockey, make some money, go back to school, and finish my education. In retrospect, considering how I struggled for a couple of years with depression, which may have been triggered partially by the fact I wouldn't be playing hockey anymore, then maybe I could have been like Ken Dryden, for example, who so successfully combined a career in hockey with a career in law. I expected that my life would have proceeded along in that direction. So, when hockey was removed from the equation, then I put all my energies into being a scientist."

"Hockey remained an important part of my life in the sense that I worked for 28 years at the Jackson Laboratory on the coast of Maine and hockey was a wonderful activity for me and my children. I continued to do that. I skated a lot, whenever I could. I was born and raised in Canada . . . you've got to love hockey."

STU McNEILL

School and hockey were two things Stu McNeill was very good at. Unlike a lot of players from his era, McNeill took his schooling very seriously. And unlike a lot of players from that era, this meant McNeill had something his fellow players didn't have: options. "My dad was a high school teacher and principal. He always insisted that I go to school. It was very difficult in those days to go to school and play hockey. In Junior A you were on the ice and travelling all the time. It was almost impossible to do both. But I did; I managed it. It was hard. I always knew I was going to continue on with my education," Stu McNeill explains.

During the 1958–59 season, McNeill got called up to the Detroit Red Wings from his Junior A team in Hamilton. On March 14, 1959, there he was in the Boston Garden, looking around the Detroit dressing room at his Red Wings teammates. When he looked around he saw faces he knew, like Howe, Delvecchio, and Sawchuk. "Most of the guys were pretty quiet. They mostly kept to themselves. There wasn't a whole lot of socializing or that kind of stuff. Sawchuk was very quiet off the ice, really quiet. He didn't say much to anybody. A lot of the guys were like that. They were hard working, honest guys."

"Gordie would say hi. But they really kept to themselves. You knew you were a rookie, for sure. They made no bones about it, there was no 'Hey, welcome to Detroit.' No way. You just sat there. But Red [Kelly] was pretty good. He went out of his way to engage in conversation. He was one of the only ones. Marcel Pronovost was very good that way, too."

That night in Boston, Stu McNeill, the kid with options, scored his first NHL goal. It came at 3:33 of a second period, over 60 years ago. "You know, I recall it pretty well," McNeill begins. "Harry Lumley was the goaltender. I was playing on a line with Alex Delvecchio and I'm not sure who the other player was. It was a good shot. I was in front of the net. I was playing centre. I was in front of the net, maybe 10 or 12 feet out. I got the puck from Alex from the side and had a nice clear shot in the corner and put it in. It was a good goal. Alex got the puck for me. I kept it. I still have it."

He does indeed still have that puck; one of Stu McNeill's patients mounted it for him. To put it more accurately, one of *Dr.* Stu McNeill's patients mounted the puck for him. When McNeill scored that night in Boston, he knew he was destined for a great career, just not on the ice. Stu McNeill knew he wanted to one day become Dr. Stu McNeill: "I knew from very early on that I was going to become a doctor. I knew that. The pro career was not, to be honest, first and foremost in my long-range plans." This wasn't something McNeill advertised to his Detroit teammates. "We didn't discuss it very much. I did a little bit with Red Kelly, I think, maybe because Red was pretty understanding."

Detroit still wanted to sign McNeill when his junior career came to an end after the 1958–59 season. He was just a call-up to the Wings from Hamilton when he scored that goal in Boston, but now Jack Adams and the Wings wanted McNeill to sign on the dotted line and embark on a pro career with the organization.

"I had been accepted to the University of Toronto medical school after my junior career. I wasn't even going to turn pro; I was going to go to medical school. Jack Adams, and Bruce Norris, who owned the Detroit Red Wings, asked my dad and I to fly down, which we did, and have a meeting. Jack said, 'Look, I'd really like you to give the pro game a try for a year or two and see if you like it or not.' I hemmed and hawed, and finally I said, 'Yes. I will give it two years.' I signed a pro contract for two years."

Just like that Stu McNeill was a pro hockey player. And almost just like that, two weeks after signing, McNeill says he knew he made the wrong choice: "I realized it was a mistake. To get fully trained as a surgeon was going to take me about 10 or 12 years. That was a long time. I thought, 'Geez, I can't delay this that much longer.' So I told Jack — who was the GM — I said, 'Mr. Adams, I really made a mistake here. I would like to go to medical school, but I realize I have to play the year out.'"

Adams and the Wings decided to let McNeill out of the second year of his contract. But like McNeill said, he did play out the first year of his deal. He was sent to Detroit's minor league team, the Edmonton Flyers. He finished his pro career with 27 points in 59 games with Edmonton. "I'm glad I did it. It wasn't for me. I loved the game, by the way, it was nothing to do with the game. I loved the game. I loved everything about hockey. I loved the physical contact. I just really wanted to get on with my education."

Stu McNeill enrolled at the University of Toronto. He played a bit of hockey, too. After a couple of years, he went and appealed to get his amateur status back. It was granted, and McNeill ended up playing with the U of T Varsity Blues. "During my medical school years I played for U of T. That was a really fun time, I really enjoyed that. I played defence, by the way, because I wasn't in very good shape. I made the All-Star Team that year," McNeill chuckles.

After 11 years McNeill left the University of Toronto. The former NHLer was now Dr. Stu McNeill, an orthopedic surgeon. He never really played hockey again; it was on to the life he always dreamed of, a life in medicine. He had a brief life as an NHLer as well. Those are two types of jobs that people dream of having. Dr. McNeill got to do both: "It's been great. It really has been. Medicine has been the most important. The most significant part of my life has been my life in medicine, but these hockey memories are great, too."

Every once in a while, one of Dr. McNeill's patients would connect the dots and discover that their surgeon was once an NHLer who played in the Original Six. "A lot of patients would do that. It was quite common actually. I met a guy the other day who grew up in Detroit. He was at the same golf course as me and he knew who I was. He had actually been to the old Olympia Stadium. We reminisced, and he remembered . . . I couldn't believe it. It's fun to talk to people like that. I really enjoy it."

Dr. Stu McNeill is a man who gave up what would have likely been a career of thrilling thousands, for a career that likely saved hundreds. He sounds very happy about his decision. Does he wonder about his "other" life? "I think I really would have enjoyed a career in hockey, too. I do. I knew Stan Mikita pretty well and Dave Keon. We were all centres together in the OHA and I knew all those guys. I saw them. I followed their careers very closely. Murray Oliver, another great player, I knew him in Hamilton. So I knew these guys as juniors and I followed them, and I thought, 'Gee, I could have done that,' but I don't regret it. But I think I could have been okay."

"That goal means a lot. In those days, there were only 90 players in the NHL. It was extremely exciting. It still does mean a lot, even to this day. It's not a really big feat when you come right down to it. But to me, it meant a lot. Still does."

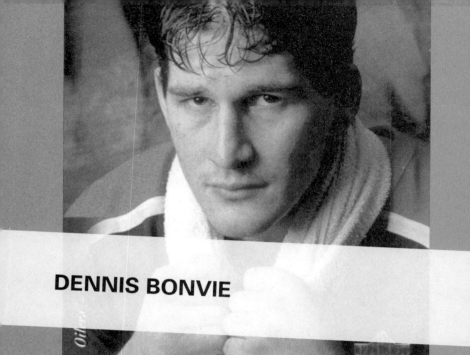

DENNIS BONVIE

When Dennis Bonvie says this, he wants one thing to be very clear: he means no disrespect to Wayne Gretzky whatsoever. "That record will never be broken. I don't want to say this out of disrespect to Wayne, but it is safer than his [points] record. Someone may challenge Wayne Gretzky, everybody is getting points all the time, but nobody gets penalty minutes anymore. Nobody gets 50 minutes [in a season] anymore. Even if you did get a hundred minutes a year, you'd have to play for 48 years."

Now when Bonvie says "that record," he means his own. In his professional hockey career he accumulated an astounding 4,804 penalty minutes. No one in the history of the game has had more. Not Tiger Williams. Not Tie Domi. Not Bob Probert. The all-time professional PIMs record belongs to Dennis Bonvie. Good luck to anyone who sets out to break that one. "Again, and I mean this, that's no disrespect to Wayne. Take it from someone who played a game or two of pro hockey — Wayne was the best player who ever lived. It's just that no one gets penalty minutes anymore."

Dennis Bonvie also scored one NHL goal. When his journey began towards those 4,804 PIMs and one NHL goal, Bonvie was just another kid in Frankville, Nova Scotia. He was not a minor hockey whiz kid. No one thought he was the next big thing. In a small place like Port Hawkesbury, NS, where Dennis played his minor hockey, kids played in age groups of two. For example, the 10- and 11-year-olds would play together and the 12- and 13-year-olds would play together: "The first year I wouldn't make the top team because it was all second-year guys. The next year I'd make it, but I'd be in the middle of the pack. I don't think there were expectations for me to play hockey at a higher level."

But Bonvie stuck with the game. He had size and he was a tough kid. He eventually worked his way onto the Antigonish Bulldogs of the Maritime Junior A Hockey League. To say the MJAHL was a tough place in the early 1990s is a vast understatement. The league was loaded with heavyweights. The toughies dropped their mitts and filled arenas from Summerside to Halifax. Some of them would never be heard from again. Some, like Bonvie, went on to bigger and better things. He eventually found his way to the OHL. First, there was a quick stop in Kitchener. His fisticuffs were top-notch; the rest of his game needed work. "Oh, I was raw," says Bonvie. "I couldn't turn one way. I had trouble crossing my feet over — it sounds funny, but I just didn't know how to do it. I played the game for fun. I got an opportunity because somebody believed in me, and I made the most of it. I kept knocking on doors until one or two opened. I did whatever I had to do to keep forging my way ahead. But I was very raw."

Eventually the North Bay Centennials picked up his OHL rights. And that is where Dennis Bonvie met the man who changed his hockey career. He'd knocked on a lot of doors; now he came face to face with the man who would give him his opportunity: the legendary Bert Templeton. Templeton was very blunt in their first meeting. "He said, 'You don't come with high credentials, kid.'"

Bonvie could have sulked; he could have gone home — he didn't. "I told him I'm going to be the toughest guy in this league. Bert said, 'What are you talking about?' I said, 'If you give me an opportunity to prove myself, I'm going to be the toughest guy in this league.' He said, 'All right,' and he just kind of shook his head."

Templeton may not have been an immediate convert that day, but what Bonvie said was enough to let Templeton give the raw kid a chance. "He dressed me for the first game. He sent me out on the ice. I fought the toughest guy on the ice. I came back to our bench, didn't say much. I did well. Then I went out again, they said the tough guys are out there. I fought again. I just kind of kept on doing it. I was getting a few shifts and playing and working my way into the lineup. I was fighting every tough guy I could to get my foot in the door. That was my ticket, so I had to do that. And I kept working on my skills to get an opportunity to play."

Bonvie found his niche in North Bay. He was *the* tough guy, but he wasn't a goal scorer. In his rookie OHL season he had 261 PIMs in 49 games with North Bay. Add in the 23 he had in seven games with Kitchener, and that was 284 PIMs for Bonvie, good enough for second in the league. In 1992–93, he led the OHL with 316 penalty minutes. He did it the only way he could. "Somebody said to me one time, 'Tie Domi fights 15 times a year and makes a lot of money. Would you like to do that?' I said, 'I'd love to do it.' He said, 'Well, then give yourself every opportunity to do that.'"

The following season, Bonvie became a pro hockey player. He began his pro career in the AHL with Cape Breton. He had 278 PIMs. He had 11 points, too, in the 63 games he played for the Baby Oilers. In his second AHL season Bonvie put up a bone-crunching 422 PIMs in 74 games. And he managed to suit up in two NHL games with Edmonton. By the time the 2001–02 season rolled around Bonvie had a reputation as one tough dude. The Bruins were the fourth NHL team he suited up for. On February 26, 2002, he played in the 61st NHL game of his career. He was still looking for his first NHL goal. The Bruins were in Uniondale, NY, to take on the Islanders. "I don't know how many games into the NHL I was, but I was pretty fearful I wasn't going to ever get a goal. You get to a certain point where you've played so many games without a goal and you think, 'I'm never going to get one.'"

This night was typical. Bonvie was not getting a ton of ice time on the fourth line. The job description was simple: keep the puck out of your net and get physical. Just under three minutes into the first, Dennis Bonvie decided to go beyond the call of duty: "Gord Murphy passed the puck up to me. I was on the wing. I caught the Islanders on a change. I came down the wing. When I was just over the blue line I let a slapshot go. I think it kind of dipped and tricked Chris Osgood. It went five-hole. I kind of went into shock after that. Benny Hogue came over and hugged me. He said, 'Hey man, nice goal. What's wrong?'"

Dennis Bonvie was out of his element. After a scrap he knew what to do. After a shift he knew what to do. But he had no idea what to do now. He had just scored his first NHL goal, and he was in the weeds. When Benoit Hogue asked Bonvie what was going on, Bonvie got right to the point: "'I never scored in the National Hockey League before . . . I don't know what to do.' It was one of those deals. You're so shocked that you scored because you didn't think it was ever going to happen."

Perhaps to ease his nerves, or maybe just to feel normal again, Bonvie got back to his usual antics on his next shift. He did not go looking for another goal. "I got back into my comfort zone on my next shift when I fought my buddy Eric Cairns. The fights were a lot easier to come by than the goals."

Bonvie had 84 PIMs in 23 games with the Bruins that year to go along with his one goal. It was the highest-scoring NHL season he ever had. It was also the most PIMs he ever had in a single NHL season. Bonvie had 311 career NHL PIMs. The other forty-five hundred or so, give or take a few majors, came in the minors. Those PIMs and that goal all came from a commitment Bonvie, the raw kid, made to himself a few years after he was playing minor hockey. "I started fighting when I was done midget and I was playing junior hockey. I went to Kitchener and then I got sent home. I played in Antigonish and I did well — a 17-year-old fighting against 19- and 20-year-olds. Then when I went to North Bay, there came a point where I wasn't sure if I was going to stay there or come back home and play college hockey. I basically decided that when I was done everything, I needed to be able to look in the mirror and be happy with myself. The only way I could do that was to give it everything I could and try to be the toughest I could be. I decided to keep working on my skills, and that's what gave me an opportunity to play in the National Hockey League."

He played in 92 career NHL games, and he scored one goal, too. And, oh yeah, there are 4,804 pro penalty minutes. It is safe to say, with way the game is played now, there will never be another Dennis Bonvie.

Courtesy of the Kamloops Blazers

ROB SKRLAC

There's an old adage I've heard over the years. I'm not sure where I first heard it, but it basically goes like this: don't let the game use you, you use the game. In other words, get as much out of the game as you can, whether you make it to high school hockey, Junior B, or the pros. That's pretty much how Rob Skrlac looked at hockey and his career: "I was just tickled to be playing in the Rocky Mountain Junior A Hockey League. Then I got to skate in Kamloops with a great franchise, got to build a relationship with one of the great GMs in hockey with Lou Lamoriello, and I got the chance to call New Jersey home," Rob Skrlac says.

Skrlac was an over-ager in the WHL during the 1996–97 season with the Kamloops Blazers. He was drafted by the Buffalo Sabres in the ninth round of the 1995 Draft but had no intention of signing with the club. Skrlac was one of the top enforcers in the "Dub." He hung right in there with one of the other heavies in the league, Scott Parker. The Devils had taken Parker in the third round of the 1996 Draft. When he wasn't dropping the gloves with Parker and the other heavies of the WHL, Skrlac spent some time that season helping out at a hockey school run by a Devils scout named Jan Ludvig, who lived in Kamloops. "That season in the Western League, it was pretty much just Scott Parker and myself. There was nobody else that could kind of hang out in that rare air, we were both just so big and strong. Frankly, Parks and I used to kick the crap out of each other. The story goes that Lou asked who can best handle Scott Parker or beat him up, and Jan said, 'I got Skrlac right here.' So, when the Sabres didn't sign me, the Devils reached out. It turned into a 15-year love affair with the New Jersey Devils."

Skrlac showed up for his first training camp with the Devils in the fall of 1997. When he looked around, there were some big boys there. Guys like Colin White, Eric Bertrand, Lyle Odelein, and the Devils' resident heavyweight, Krzysztof Oliwa. "[Lou] wasn't trying to crack any atoms, that's for sure. But he was trying to crack some skulls, I think," Skrlac laughs.

Skrlac and Oliwa had spent some time working out together during the summer: "He knew what I was there to do, and I knew what he had been there to do." In his first scrimmage at camp, Skrlac was on one team and Oliwa was on the other. "We had trained together for about six, seven weeks, but Ollie smashed into a kid named Wes Mason. Wes was a small guy. It was right in front of the scout's box. I thought, 'Well, I can't let that go.' So I went and I fought Ollie and I did really well against him. He made the NHL that year and I kind of filled in the hole he left in Albany."

There were no hard feelings: Oliwa and Skrlac even went to lunch the next day. Rob Skrlac was off to Albany. He would spend the large majority of the next decade playing in the AHL for the River Rats. Unlike a lot of minor-leaguers, he did not move around. He stuck with the Devils. He was content in his minor league role. He liked the Devils and they liked him. When I ask him why, he says: "Loyalty. There was just a consistency with the philosophy, the discipline. It really matched up with the type of organization I wanted to be involved with and I had a strong relationship with a guy named John Cunniff. He was our head coach in Albany. John and I would meet back at the rink at two o'clock and we'd spend two hours boxing and working out together. This is a 55-year-old man who's picking up pretty much the same weights I am. I knew I was only ever going to play two to four minutes a night, based on my skill set, but I understood that, and I chose to become very proficient at what got me there."

Skrlac put his head down and went to work. Work meant a whole lot of working out and sticking up for teammates, but as he said, not a ton of ice time. In his first pro season with the River Rats, Skrlac spent 256 minutes in the penalty box and didn't score a single goal. The next season, he had 213 minutes and one goal: "People chuckle when I tell them this, but I've probably had one bar fight my whole life. It's really not who I am, but I was able to become a specialist in that role and understand that it was a job. And it was a great job. Somebody paid me to work out 12 months out of the year and to travel around with 20 of my best friends on a bus or on a plane. I relished it."

By the time he was 24, Skrlac, as he says himself, went from "prospect to suspect. I was making a lot of money for a fourth-line tough guy." The Devils signed a 20-year-old player named Brett Clouthier. "Clouts came in and he was big and strong. He even scored a couple of goals, which I just couldn't figure out how to do, as much as I wanted to and as much as I tried to."

The Devils sent Skrlac down to the Mississippi Sea Wolves of the ECHL. He eventually landed back in the AHL with the Portland Pirates: "I played with Mel Angelstad, Stephen Peat. We had a tough team there. It was awesome."

Towards the end of the season the Pirates were set to face off against Skrlac's old Albany team: "Before the game, I told [Portland coach] Glen Hanlon: 'As soon as they put Clouthier on the ice, make sure that I get out there.' I remember Hanlon said, 'He's the guy who took your job, right?' 'Yep.' He looked at me for a second. 'Done.'"

"So, I go out there. Clouts was young, and I probably scared him a bit, but I ended up making him look pretty bad. I consider Brett a friend. I played with him; I respect him. But I had a single message I wanted to send to the Devils."

New Jersey got the message. Just after the season ended Skrlac was packing up his stuff, getting ready to head home for the summer, when his phone rang. "It was the Devils. They asked me to stop off in New Jersey when I was driving home. Lou invited me into his office. I sat near his desk and he said, 'No, let's go sit on the couch, kid.' We had a chat and he said, 'Rob, I made a mistake. There's still a home here for you. I would like you to think about coming back.' I didn't even think about it. We shook hands right there and I signed a contract at the end of June with the Devils and I was back home again."

The next season Skrlac went back to work in Albany. It was a typical Rob Skrlac year. He had two goals and 165 PIMs in 45 games. The next season, Skrlac went back to work again. This time things were a little different. Skrlac was at Devils camp on a pro tryout. He did not have a deal with the Devils. But something clicked: "I had a good training camp. On the last day of camp when we were all packing up to go to Albany, I got a ring. It was Lou's secretary. She said, 'Do you have a minute for the big guy?' I said, 'Absolutely.' I had fought Todd Fedoruk the night before, and Pat Burns played me about 12, maybe 15 minutes — the most ice I have ever gotten."

That and all the years Skrlac put in with his franchise were enough to impress Lou Lamoriello. The secretary put the GM on the phone. "Lou told me, 'Well, you did it.' And I said, 'I did what?' He said, 'You did it. You're going to play in the NHL.' He added, 'I don't know how quickly this is going to happen. I have to make some roster moves.'"

The Devils signed Skrlac to an American League contract. He was in Albany again, but with the promise of a promotion to New Jersey. Just before Christmas in 2003, 26-year-old Rob Skrlac was called up to the NHL for the first time. He can thank, in part, a Philadelphia tough guy who was running around the ice one night in the first game of a back-to-back against New Jersey: "Donald Brashear was running around. He was chasing Scott Stevens around and kind of being an ass — that is, doing exactly what the Flyers paid him to do. Lou was very unhappy with that, so they called me up."

Skrlac dressed for his first NHL game on December 13, 2003. There were no fireworks from the veteran American League tough guy. He didn't fight. He didn't take a penalty. He didn't score. But he sure was happy: "I played 23 seconds and I got a feature article in the *NHL All-Star* magazine. Somebody wrote a story in Philadelphia about how it took me 26 years to play 23 seconds in the NHL and that I couldn't stop smiling about it."

"It was more about the journey and less about the destination. It took all those years and all those stitches and all those extra workouts. Maybe a cliché, but I was known as the first guy on the ice and the last guy off the ice."

Skrlac could not stop smiling. He was somewhere he never expected to be — in the NHL. After that first game and his 23 seconds of ice time, Skrlac headed to the Devils bus. He was still smiling. "You really want to understand the character of Scott Stevens? I only played 23 seconds, and I remember the reporter asking me about it. I was just so positive and pleased to be there, which is why he wrote the article the way he did. I wasn't bitching about it. It was amazing. I worked my whole life to be here. I'm sitting on the bus to drive back to Jersey from Philadelphia, and Scottie was the first guy to get on. He walks up to me and he stops. He shook my hand and said, 'Congratulations, Robbie. You deserve this.'"

Skrlac's smile got even bigger five nights later in Atlanta. That was the night the kid who, once upon a time, was just happy to play Junior A in the Rocky Mountain league scored in the best league in the world. His ice time for that night? Forty-six seconds.

"Look — I doubled my ice time. What an improvement. I think I had two shifts that night."

"I was playing with Erik Rasmussen and, I believe, Mike Rupp. We dumped the puck in and I went in the corner. I can't remember the defenceman's name, he was a relatively tough guy, and I figured, 'Well, I better get some penalty minutes here,' so I was asking him to fight. He wouldn't do it, so I skated back to the front of the net. And just as I do that, Rassie comes around the top of the left-hand circle and he just puts it on net and it goes off either my stick or my leg, and I say 'either' because the video wasn't all digital back then. Initially they gave the goal to Rasmussen. I was very excited because I got a plus in the NHL."

Things were about to change. Up in the broadcast booth for the Devils that night was John Hennessy. He knew Skrlac well. When Skrlac played in Albany, Hennessy was the River Rats play-by-play announcer. Now Hennessy was the play-by-play announcer for the Devils. "John was sitting beside the NHL video booth. During the break he said, 'Hey, do you guys have a second? Can you rewind that video and see if it touched Skrlac?' And they determined the puck hit my shin pad. I thought it hit my stick, at least I'll tell my kids that. They went back to Toronto and broke it down, and during the intermission they awarded me the goal."

Skrlac didn't find out until after the game. He didn't get a chance to raise his stick in the air. Instead he celebrated in the Devils dressing room. "Grant Marshall had pulled his groin in the morning skate, which is why I got to play that night. Marshy comes bursting through the door with the game puck with my name on it. 'You got the fucking game-winning goal!' I just sat there. 'Marshy, you're fucking with me.' 'No, Robbie. It happened.' And the boys are dying. Everyone is saying, 'First shot, first goal, game winner. It's like what? Mario Lemieux, Wayne Gretzky, Rob Skrlac.'"

Now, maybe you're thinking that getting a goal off your shin pad is a fluke. But it is not. Rob Skrlac needed to know where to go on the ice for the chance to deflect a puck. Years of being on the ice at practice, being the first guy on, the last guy off, had paid off. But there was more to it. "It really comes down to positioning. And it's not the positioning of knowing to go to the front of the net, because I'm bigger than everybody else. It's about knowing that I could not eat that extra cheeseburger in the summertime. I had to measure my food and I had to do that second and third workout every fucking day or I was never going to get a chance to ever play."

"I [always said], 'Well, I made it this far. Let's see how much farther I can go.' I'm getting chills just talking about it. I love it."

Skrlac spent another six games with the Devils. He got his last taste of NHL action in Atlanta as well. On January 25th, he played another 46 seconds against the Thrashers. He didn't score that night, but he did drop the gloves with Francis Lessard. The next season, the lockout came, perhaps costing Skrlac another chance at some time in the NHL. "Unfortunately, as I made the NHL the incumbent millionaires decided they weren't rich enough and went on strike. It was really painful for a lot of guys in my shoes. Guys like Doug Doull; guys like Mel Angelstad; guys who finally got their foot in the door and played a game or two and proved to the world that they could do it . . . and then all of a sudden, there's no more league. And then they change all the rules, and now we're left with hockey that, frankly, I don't even watch anymore."

Skrlac spent the lockout season in the AHL and then went to work for the Devils as a team ambassador. He spoke anywhere from 150 to 200 times a year, telling his story. It was the story of how a kid from a logging town on North Vancouver Island ("the first eight years of my life we lived in a logging camp; we didn't even have a store") managed to make it all the way to the NHL and score a goal in the best hockey league in the world.

"It was always the same message. No matter how hard it seems, no matter how unlikely it seems, if I can do it, there's no reason that you can't achieve your dreams." And while Skrlac was working for the Devils he also completed his business degree. He stuck with the Devils for as long as Lou Lamoriello did. When Lamoriello, who gave him his job off the ice with Jersey, left for Toronto, Skrlac left Jersey as well. He moved to Alberta, where he works in the oil and gas sector: "I was always flattered that Lou thought highly of me, and I was kind of amazed with the opportunities that he offered me."

The kid who was simply thrilled to get a team sweatsuit when he played in the Rocky Mountain League at 17 got as much out of the game as he could.

CHRIS McRAE

When the Detroit Red Wings and the Philadelphia Flyers faced off on April 1, 1990, there wasn't much on the line for either team. It was the final game of the regular season. The Wings weren't going to the playoffs. The Flyers weren't going to the playoffs. In terms of intensity, this wasn't exactly going to rival the seventh game of a Stanley Cup Final. But, in terms of opportunity, it was a perfect scenario for veteran minor league tough guy Chris McRae: "Neither team was motivated to win. They were out of the playoffs, we were out of the playoffs, and whoever won would get a higher pick in the draft."

Chris McRae found himself in the Wings starting lineup. He was on a line with another tough guy, Kevin McClelland, and the late Shawn Burr. McRae lined up opposite Philadelphia power forward Rick Tocchet. "He kind of looks at me and says, 'So, Chris, how do you want to play it?' I said, 'Any way you want, Rick. I'm just here trying to fit in.' And he says, 'Well, you know what, why don't we just play hard and hit each other? Just play hard. You're getting a shot here to play. You need the ice time more than I do.'"

The tone was set. And by that I mean Chris McRae didn't have to set the tone. There was no need to drop the gloves. The Wings and Flyers were going to keep it clean and get through the final 60 minutes of their seasons unscathed, if possible. That afternoon Detroit rolled all four lines, which meant that McRae got more NHL ice time than he had in his previous 20 NHL games. Just over seven and a half minutes into the first period — it happened. "We just came up through the neutral zone. I moved the puck to Shawn Burr. McClelland went to the net. I was in the high slot. Shawn made a nice saucer pass. He just laid the puck there so I could one-time it. I just pounded it home."

"I was in shock, quite frankly. I couldn't believe it went in. I curled off and came back to the bench. It was funny, the guys were all happy for me. They knew it was my first NHL goal. They were kind of emptying the bench. Joey Kocur came over the boards and he goes, 'Fuck yeah, McRae.'"

Chris McRae hardly moved. He was in a state of disbelief. There was no fist-pumping. He didn't wave his hands in the air. If he wasn't going to milk it, his coach was going to at least give him a chance to soak it up. "The coach said to my line, 'Go back to centre ice and take the faceoff.' We go back to centre ice. I was almost kind of embarrassed. Like, 'Holy fuck.'"

McRae went to line up for the draw. The magic of the moment may have been lost on him. He may have been in a state of shock. But once again, the guy opposite him on the draw broke the ice. "Tocchet leaned over and discreetly said, 'Is that your first?' 'Yeah.' Rick said, '*Ever?*' 'Yeah.' 'Hey, congratulations.'"

Once the shock wore off, McRae must have enjoyed the feeling of scoring an NHL goal. He wanted more. He just kept going to the net. If he got a bounce just an inch or two the other way that night, there was no way he would ever have made it into this book. "I hit the crossbar and the post in that same game. I could have had three goals. Doug Houda was my roommate that road trip and he said to me afterwards, 'Man, you were all over the net.'"

All these years later, that post and that crossbar kind of come in handy. The goal McRae scored that day in Philly came on his only shot on goal of the year. In fact, it came on the only shot on goal of his career. (Hitting the post or a crossbar is not an official shot on goal.) McRae finished his 21-game NHL career with a career shooting percentage of 100. "There's a statistic where I have the best shooting percentage in hockey because I only took one shot on net [in his career]."

April 1, 1990, was not your typical Chris McRae game. He was a tough guy. He fought — a lot. He spent 290 minutes in an AHL penalty box in '89–'90. He racked up another 45 PIMs in the NHL that year. He did not fight that day: "It was a fun game to play in because it was a very relaxed game. When you fight a lot, and I fought a lot, you're usually a little more antsy, because of your role. That game was kind of like flag football."

That wasn't usually the case for McRae. And yes, if you're wondering, Chris's older brother Basil was a tough guy as well. Basil spent 2,453 minutes in an NHL penalty box. In the third game of Chris's NHL career, a little over two years before he scored his goal, Chris, then with the Leafs, faced off against Basil, then with the North Stars, for the only time in his NHL career. The brothers' parents had made the drive down to Toronto from their hometown of Beaverton, Ontario, "probably in some shitty car," Chris tells me.

When Mom and Dad looked down on the Maple Leaf Gardens ice that night, they saw their two boys, Chris and Basil, lined up at centre ice for the opening faceoff. They were right beside one another. The McRae boys had already played against each other in the American League, but this was the big time. "Basil came over on his off-wing. We were both left-wingers, so we wouldn't naturally line up against each other, but we did at that faceoff. Maybe he thought someone would take a picture of us and give it to our parents. I don't know what he was thinking. But he came over. He leaned over to me and he said, 'Hey, don't fuck around in the shower afterwards, get out quick. Mom and Dad have to get back up to the farm in that fucking car they're driving.' The puck drops and he said, 'Good luck.'"

Maybe from the stands or on TV it looked like they were talking about more than just their parents. Maybe the odd fan or even the odd player thought the McRae boys were going to go. "When I came back to the bench, Russ Courtnall asked me, 'Are you and Bas going to go? Are you guys yapping at each other?' And I replied, 'No, he just told me to hurry up after the game. Mom and Dad gotta get home.'"

That was the only time Chris and Basil shared the ice that night: "I had no interest in fighting my brother," says Chris. At least not for fun. But if Basil did cross the line, he'd be treated like any other opposing player. "If he did something on the ice and I had to go in and grab him, I would have fought him. I wouldn't have suckered him or done anything dirty. If he said, 'Let's go,' I would have fought. Quite frankly, if he would have said, 'Let's fight, it will be good to get you publicity,' I would have fought him. But I wouldn't say, 'Hey, come on, let's fight.' My father would just sit there and watch, but I don't think my mom would have been too happy about that."

Chris McRae fought until the very end of his hockey career. About two years after he scored that goal in Philly he played his final professional game. He spent his final season in the International League and he didn't exactly fade into the sunset: 413 penalty minutes in a mere 60 games. He spent a lot of time playing with future NHL coach Bruce Boudreau. Back in those days Boudreau was a more than reliable minor league goal scorer. McRae gave him a ton of room on the ice: "I used to say to Gabby before every game, 'If anybody touches you, Gabby, I'm going to fuckin' kill them.' He loved it. He used to say to me, 'Go early. I love it when you go early.' I got into this rhythm where I used to fight the first shift of every game," McRae laughs.

But at the end of that season, McRae packed it in. He took some night courses, got his securities licence, and decided to hang them up. "I thought: I'm 27 years old. I haven't made the NHL on a full time basis. I'm probably not going to make it. I kept thinking, 'Don't be a hockey bum, don't be a hockey bum. Move on.'"

McRae had his post-playing career plan in place. Unlike a lot of players, he knew what he wanted to do. He was going to enter the financial world. That, however, did not mean the transition from hockey player to nine-to-fiver was going to be easy.

"I was very depressed. Even though I felt I was doing the right thing, I would look at myself and my reflection on the subway when I'd come back from night school and I didn't like it. I kept thinking I wanted to go back and play hockey. But I kept saying if you go back then you're sort of procrastinating and deferring the inevitable. Do I think I would have gone back and made it to the NHL? No."

"In hindsight now, as a guy in my fifties, I think you should play the game for as long as you can because it is a long time that you don't play it."

It's been more than a quarter century since Chris McRae played his last pro game. He spends his days working in Toronto's financial district. He's a long way from that goal he scored on April Fool's Day, 1990. Chris McRae got into 14 NHL fights in his career. He had many more in the minors. He made his hockey living the hard way. And when it was all said and done, he scored one NHL goal, in pretty much the only game of his career when he didn't have to play the tough guy role: "It was kind of *carpe diem* — seize the day. They just rolled four lines that day. It was almost like being a kid again. Instead of sitting there on the bench being a hired assassin, you actually got to go out and feel the puck and handle the puck. Not that Rick Tocchet was going to let you off the hook or anything. But Tocchet basically said, 'Hey, let's play.'"

FRANK BEATON

"I did it the old-fashioned way, and you don't do that by losing fights," says Frank Beaton. Beaton was not drafted. He was not a big-time prospect. In his second year of professional hockey he scored four goals in 65 games for the International League's Flint Generals. He made it to the NHL, just as he says, the old-fashioned way: he earned it. You name them, Frank fought them. One season he led the Southern League in penalty minutes. Another year he led the WHA in penalty minutes. His old-fashioned ways paid off when he made it all the way to Broadway with the New York Rangers.

"It was quite an experience, and of all places, to be on Broadway, in New York City, I was really awestruck. It was an unbelievable experience. Sometimes I look back and I wish that I may have played with a less glamorous team. We had Phil Esposito, Ron Duguay, John Davidson, Walter Tkaczuk, and Don Maloney. Look at the guys on that team. And the notoriety that team had, to play there, it was kind of like, 'Oh, shit.' You were under a microscope."

The bright lights of Broadway were about as glamorous as things could get for a kid from Brierly Brook, Antigonish County, Nova Scotia. Frank Beaton's hockey beginnings were not glamorous. "I lived on a farm. I did not skate on an indoor hockey rink until I was 11 years old. I went into Antigonish to play, and I was one of the two or three country kids who would come into town once a week on Saturday mornings to play with the kids from town."

With the help of some fine men from Antigonish, Beaton eventually made his way to Junior A hockey. He played for the Dartmouth Lakers when he was only 15 years old, lining up against future NHLers like Hilliard Graves and Bobby MacMillan. The next season Beaton found himself back home in Antigonish playing Junior B for the Bulldogs. And then he got his break. A man named Pete Poyer decided to put together a local senior team. He asked Beaton, who was only 16, to play with the men. "Hell yeah, I wanted to play. I didn't care who I played with, absolutely. So I'd play senior hockey against the Glace Bay Miners and the Sydney Millionaires."

One night during a game in Glace Bay, Nova Scotia, Beaton was spotted by a bird dog for the Montreal Junior Canadiens. The Frank Beaton that scout saw and invited to a Junior Canadiens camp was a different player than the one fans would see later. "I played an aggressive and hard-hitting style. I very rarely fought."

Beaton jumped on the invite to Montreal. He never caught on with the Junior Canadiens. He ended up in Sarnia, Ontario, for a year, followed by another year in junior. Undrafted, Beaton attended Atlanta Flames camp in 1973. By that time he had evolved into the Frank Beaton who took no prisoners out on the ice: "That first year in Sarnia I had a couple of fights and I did pretty well. Then it became a situation where if you can do this they start leaning on you to do it. I became the 'go-to' guy. If we were playing somebody and someone on the other team was doing things, the whole bench would look at me and say, 'Frank, you're not going to let him do this, are you?' And then of course with my obligation to the team, so to speak, I thought, 'Well, no, I won't let him get away with that.' I started fighting in Sarnia. My point is, I made those teams not because I was a fighter, but based on my ability to play hockey and score goals. And then I evolved into my role. As it turned out, it would be as the team's enforcer. So, that's how that started."

Beaton did what he could at that Flames camp, but he never caught on. "I never got a sniff from the Atlanta Flames."

But he did catch on with a pro team. His junior coach from Windsor, Jerry Serviss, had moved on to the pros with the Flint Generals. He wanted Beaton on his team. Flint was the first professional stop of Frank Beaton's career. He spent his first two professional years there. Eventually Beaton was shipped out of Flint, and that's when word of him made its way to another Antigonish County legend. "After my second year in Flint they wanted to trade me. Don Perry, who was the coach of Saginaw, tried to trade for me. Flint wouldn't trade me to Saginaw because we were in the same division. Flint traded me to Columbus."

That did not sit well with Don Perry. He was sick of having to play against Frank Beaton. If Beaton couldn't play for his team, he wasn't going to play in the International League at all. Perry picked up the phone and called an old teammate from his Eastern League days. It was a guy he knew was always looking for another tough guy. Don Perry called John Brophy. "Perry told Brophy, 'I don't want to play against him anymore. I tried to get him on my team. You gotta get him. You gotta get this guy out of here.'"

John Brophy had never heard of Frank Beaton. But he liked what Perry was saying about the mystery man. He liked the stories of his toughness. He liked the numbers he put up, too. And he liked where Beaton was from. "So, Brophy being from Antigonish County, and me being from Antigonish County, [he] decided to call me. I was at home in Brierly Brook when he called. This was after I was notified I was traded to Columbus. When Brophy called me, he said if I played for him he could get me a tryout with the Cincinnati Stingers in the WHA. I thought, 'Wow, that's a no-brainer. I'm going to go try out for Brophy.' I figured if I didn't make the Stingers in the WHA I'd end up playing for Brophy in the Southern Hockey League. Obviously I knew who John Brophy was, everybody did."

A few months later, Beaton made his way to training camp and met the legend himself. "I checked into training camp and I checked into my room at the hotel. Now remember, I had never met Broph and he had never seen me. There was a knock at the door. So I answered the door and John Brophy was there with a guy named Ian MacKinnon. Brophy looks at me and he says, 'Frank Beaton?' I had my shorts on, I was watching TV by myself in my room. I said, 'Yeah.' And Broph looked at me, and I don't know what he was expecting, or what he was expecting to see based on what he had heard about me, but he looked at me and he said, 'Where the fuck is the rest of ya!?' It was classic John Brophy. The first thing I thought was, 'Aw, fuck. What kind of chance do I have?' I was 175 pounds soaking wet. He was expecting somebody fuckin' six-foot-two, 205 pounds. I said, 'No, this is all I got.'"

And that was the beginning of an incredible lifelong relationship between the two guys from Antigonish County. Brophy, the hardened pro, the old-school coach, was the teacher. Beaton was the student. "I thought I was in shape when I met Broph. And I was. I could go with anybody. But I was kidding myself. We would practise for an hour, an hour and a half, everybody's ass would be dragging. And then he'd say, 'Okay, Beaton, get your shorts on, get your running shoes. We're not through.' I said, 'What the fuck is he talking about?' He had a heavy bag hanging outside the locker room, just down the hall a little bit where there was a little bit of room, and a speed bag, too. And he'd have me go for another 45 minutes on the heavy bag, then the speed bag, then push-ups. You name it. When I got there I thought I was in shape. I had no idea of the level of conditioning that a man could reach until I met John Brophy. He brought me to another level. He said, 'You wanna play? This is what you do.'"

"The guy was unbelievable — he was such a motivator. He was the reason I got to play. And it wasn't halfway through the season that I got called up to Cincinnati in the World Hockey Association. I owe anything that I accomplished in my career to John Brophy."

Between the WHA and Southern League, Beaton put up a combined 337 PIMs in 1975–76. He scored 19 goals, too. His toughness was turning heads and attracting the attention of the hockey world. Even the refs wanted to see Frank Beaton dance: "I remember Bill Friday, the famous NHL referee who jumped over to the WHA. He'd be reffing, you'd be jawing back and forth with a guy, and you'd have no intention of going and Friday would yell, 'Come on, you guys. If you're going to fight, drop 'em and fight. Come on. Let's go. Stop with the bullshit. If you're gonna fight, fight!'"

The 175-pound kid from Brierly Brook, who played a hard-hitting game as a teenager and scored his share of goals, too, was now the guy who was being counted upon by his teammates to mix it up at a moment's notice. He was now one of the toughest men in pro hockey. That came with a weight. "There were times, I will tell you, when I was sick and friggin' tired of it. If your mind is not in it, your body is not going to be in it. Everything follows your mind. Toughness is a state of mind. Your mind tells your body how much abuse it will allow it to take. If your mind won't let your body take a certain number of punches to the head, or a broken lip or a black eye or whatever, then your mind will shut it down and say that's it, you've had enough. You're not going to do it. And there were times that I fought when it was conflicting with what I was telling myself. And there were other times when you fight and you start to get all the accolades from it. And you start to get the press. And honestly, you start to relish it. That becomes part of your persona. And that's what you gotta live up to. There were times that I would think, 'Geez, I'm so sick of this shit.'"

Beaton may have thought that from time to time, but he kept doing his thing on the ice. The next few seasons saw Beaton continue to score and rack up an astounding number of penalty minutes. He had a league-high 274 PIMs for the WHA's Edmonton Oilers in '76–'77. The next season he played for one of the most notorious outfits in hockey history: the 1977–78 Birmingham Bulls under Glen Sonmor. Beaton played on a team with Dave Hanson, Steve Durbano, and Gilles Bilodeau. Beaton had 15 points and 259 penalty minutes in 59 games. He spent most of the next year in the AHL with the New Haven Nighthawks. He spent another 319 minutes in the box. And for the first time ever, that year, he got a taste of the NHL when he played in two games with the Rangers. The following season, Beaton spent a couple of months on Broadway when he suited up for 23 games with the Rangers. The fights, the bruises, the punches given and taken, the mental toll, finally paid off. Frank Beaton was an NHLer.

And, in Vancouver on January 23, 1980, it happened. Frank Beaton, the guy who never quit, scored his one and only NHL goal. "I kid people when I say I picked up the puck behind my own net. I went down and I deked everybody and I split the defence and went in on a breakaway, and it was so easy I went back into my own end and did it again. Obviously those kind of stories are for drinking beer and tellin' lies. The truth is I got a rebound in front of the net, and just like you're supposed to do, you backhand it toward the goalie. I missed the goalie and it went in the net."

"When it went in I thought, 'Did I get it or did somebody tip it? Am I going to get credit for this thing?' I was thinking, 'Did I really get this goal?' Well, yes I did. And what was I thinking at that point in time? A lot of people score goals in the National Hockey League then and now and they think this is just the first one. They think they're going to get 20. They think they're going to get 30. They think they're going to get 50. I knew that was outside the realm of any kind of reasonable expectation for me. For me to get that one was obviously pretty friggin' special."

Beaton was 26 years old and seven years and lots of bruises into his pro career when he scored on Glen Hanlon in that 6–4

Rangers win. He was a long way from where he started. "I'm very, very proud that I am the first guy from Antigonish County to score a goal in the National Hockey League. I'm very proud of that. Now, I only got one, I know that, and there were some great hockey players that came behind me like Craig MacDonald, Paul MacLean, and there were some guys who scored a bunch of goals in the National Hockey League, but I got the first one."

And then there is the matter of his nickname . . . we *have to* talk about the nickname "Never." That was Frank's nickname — or so they say. "The fact is, nobody ever called me Never. Never as in Frank 'Never' Beaton. John Brophy called me Beater. That was my nickname, and it still is my nickname. I do know that Bill Chadwick, the Rangers announcer, came up with a name for me out of the blue one night, but he called me Seldom, as in Seldom Beaton. He thought that was pretty clever. Then someone, fans or whatever, took it to Never Beaton."

The Legend of Frank "Never" Beaton grew thanks to the man himself. Like a lot of folks from down in the Maritimes, Frank Beaton can hold an audience captive. The man is witty and can tell a story. A few years after the WHA came to an end, Frank Beaton decided to tell a little tale about himself at a WHA reunion. Frank was interviewed by a reporter and asked about the nickname. "I didn't know what to say, so I thought, 'All right, I'll get a little cute here.' I said, 'I don't know how I got started with Never, but all of a sudden it was Seldom and then it became Always and then I quit.' That was my attempt at self-deprecation and trying to be funny, but then that story grew legs."

Never, Seldom, Always. Frank says to just call him Beater. Beater, the kid who went all the way from Brierly Brook, Antigonish County, to the bright lights of Broadway. "I'm very fucking proud that I got to score one goal in the National fucking Hockey League. They can't take it away from me. It's recorded. They'll never take it away from me. I did it. I scored a goal."

Acknowledgements

First, I would like to thank the thirty-nine men who shared their stories to make this book possible: I enjoyed each and every one. In most cases, they took the time to answer a random phone call from a stranger. I thank them for all they shared, their openness and honesty, and I thank them for allowing me to understand — as a kid who always dreamed of scoring in the NHL — what the moment actually means, and the legacy it creates.

A special thank you to my good friend Colby Armstrong. I always loved him as a player, and I love him as a broadcaster, too. But I love him even more as a friend. When you hear the phrase "salt of the earth," think of Colby Armstrong. He had a fantastic career and will always be the King of the Half Clapper.

As per usual the folks at ECW have been outstanding. Thank you Michael Holmes, Shannon Parr, Peter Norman, Jessica Albert, Emily Ferko, Susannah Ames, Aymen Saidane, David Caron, and Jack David. Thank you all for making this book possible. Thank you all for making books.

My literary agent, Brian Wood, was at the forefront when it came to turning an idea into the pages you see before you. Thanks, once again, Brian: now please update your blog.

So many people helped make this book possible. People like Sportsnet Stats guru Steve Fellin, who looked up the initial list of one goal scorers for me when I pondered this idea a couple of years ago. Speaking of Sportsnet, once again they have been beyond supportive when it comes to my writing. Thanks Jon Coleman, Rob Corte, Jeff Marek, Tim and Sid, Evanka Osmak, Ron MacLean, Ryan Moynes, Elliotte Friedman, Paul Bromby, Arash Madani, Jeff Azzopardi, Jeff Blair, Stephen Brunt, Rich Choi, Dave Cadeau, Sportsnet The Fan 590, Meghann Cox, and Brendan Dunlop.

One of the cool things about doing a book like this is playing detective and trying to track down all these goal scorers. So many people helped with that, and also contributed to this book in other ways. So thank you Tim Boyce, Brent Krahn, Terry Ryan, Todd Warriner, Dr. Grant Roberts, Paul Patskou, Lenard Kotylo, Scott Thomas, Jay Noble, David Salter, The Hutchman, Andre Brin, Nick Hart, Troy Shanks, Chris Carlin and Upper Deck, Warren Kosel, Gerry Liscumb, Donald McMillan, Glenn Healy, Jackson Houck, Scott Gray, Darren Burns, Uncle Jesse Duke, Charles Henri Landry, Andrew Jackson and Bob Clarke of Jackson Events, Billy Duke, Steve Thomas, and Jordy Douglas.

As always, the resources of hockeydb.com, hockey-reference.com., and NHL.com were beyond valuable.

And of course, none of this happens without the support of my family. To my beautiful wife, who never wants her name to appear in print: I love you, Mrs. Reid. Thank you for everything, including the ultimate definition of everything, our boys Cobs and Lou. My parents have always supported my passion for the game of hockey. Thanks Mom and Dad and Barry and Carolyn, too. And thanks to my sister Kate and brother Peter who have been by my side forever.

And finally, thank you. Thank you for buying this book. Buying a book and sitting down and reading is an investment of your time: thanks for making me a part of it.

Purchase the print edition and receive the eBook free. Just send an email to ebook@ecwpress.com and include:

- the book title
- the name of the store where you purchased it
- your receipt number
- your preference of file type: PDF or ePub

A real person will respond to your email with your eBook attached. And thanks for supporting an independently owned Canadian publisher with your purchase!